The British South Africa Police

Origins and Early History
1885 to 1901

Wilfred Bernard Bussy
Regt. No. 1084, B.S.A.P.

TSL Publications

The Great War in Africa Association

Published in Great Britain in 2020
By Great War in Africa Association, TSL Publications, Rickmansworth

First edition, Edited and arranged in Booklet format by John Berry (5584) July, 2007, 2nd edition 2010
Published by the British South Africa Police Regimental Association (United Kingdom Branch).

This edition, Copyright © 2020 British South Africa Police Regimental Association (United Kingdom Branch)

Photographs Courtesy Cliff Rogers and National Archives of Zimbabwe.

ISBN: 978-1-913294-32-8

The right of Wilfred Bernard Bussy to be identified as the author of this work has been asserted by the editor in accordance with the UK Copyright, Designs and Patents Act 1988.

All rights reserved. No part of this publication may be reproduced, stored in a retrieval system or transmitted, in any form or by any means without the prior written permission of the publisher, nor be otherwise circulated in any form of binding or cover other than that in which it is published and without a similar condition being imposed on the subsequent buyer.

Acknowledgement and thanks go to:
The Police Review, issues of which are held at the National Army Museum.
Cliff Rogers (4735) for research at N.A.M. and for the arduous task of scanning the History from the various issues of the *Police Review*.
Alan Stock (6063) Editor of *The Outpost*, 1966 to 1984
Alan Toms (7391) Designer of the Series' cover.
The History Section Committee, UK Branch Regimental Association, under the chairmanship of Alan Toms

Apology is made for standard of some photographs. This is caused by scanning from old magazines with poor paper quality

Names of places and persons are as used by Bussy and may differ from later usage. The language of the day has been retained for cultural study purposes.

CONTENTS

Chapter 1	Birth of the B.P.P.	9
Chapter 2	The Charges of the W.M.S.	13
Chapter 3	Tribal Wars	17
Chapter 4	The Great Trek	21
Chapter 5	An Insult to the Flag	25
Chapter 6	Dutch Aspirations	29
Chapter 7	Victoria Massacre	33
Chapter 8	A Regrettable Incident	37
Chapter 9	Official Appreciation	41
Chapter 10	Capt. Coventry's Report	45
Chapter 11	The War Ended	50
Chapter 12	The Start of the Raid	55
Chapter 13	The Absent Convoy	60
Chapter 14	Dr Jameson and his Officers Sentenced	65
Chapter 15	The Withdrawal of the M.M.P.	70
Chapter 16	'Let us do some more Killing'	74
Chapter 17	The Attempted Relief of Mr Graham	77
Chapter 18	Some Laager Prices	81
Chapter 19	Lieut. Chesnaye's Escape	84
Chapter 20	The Gwaai Patrol	87
Chapter 21	Inspection by General Carrington	101
Chapter 22	The Matopos	107
Chapter 23	The Inugu Gorge	112
Chapter 24	The Modern B.SA.P.	117
Chapter 25	A Great Task for the Police	122
Chapter 26	Plumer's Task	126
Chapter 27	Deedepoort	132
Chapter 28	The Romance of Empire	138
Chapter 29	The Importance of Mafeking	143
Chapter 30	The Bombardment Begins	150
Chapter 31	A Reverse	158
Chapter 32	'Mafficking'	166

Map British South Africa Co's territories	3
Appendix One: South African War (Tomlinson)	173
Appendix Two: Nominal Roll, B.S.A.C.P. 1889/90	176

List of Photographs.
1. B.B.P. Maxim gun and crew
2. Macloutsie Camp
3. Police Tents, Tuli
4. Matabele envoys – Tuli
5. Officers of B.S.A. Co. Police, 1890
6. Fort Salisbury Camp
7. Capture of Portuguese Camp
8. 'C' Troop, Salisbury Column
9. Capt. Lendy and Fort Victoria Police
10. Khama's levies
11. Maxim gun in action – 1893
12. Parade at Fort Victoria Courthouse
13. The Victoria Rangers
14. Capt. P.W. Forbes and staff
15. Khami River fort lookout
16. Dr. Jameson and party, Pretoria gaol
17. Malema Camp
18. Native Police
19. Bulawayo Laager
20. Alderson and Godley
21. Artillery Troop – Matabeleland Division
22. Artillery Troop – Mashonaland Division
23. B.S.A.P. Squadron 1900
24. Maxim gun company – Imperial Bushmen
25. B.S.A.P. Post, Boer War
26. Heliographing from Limestone Fort to Cannon Kopje

The Author

Wilfred Bernard Bussy (known in family circles as 'Tubby') was born 23 July 1884 at Lambeth, one of four children of Bernard Bussy who, on the 1901 Census return, gave his profession as journalist and author. The author joined the B.S.A.P. on 3 July 1909, Regimental Number 1084, and was discharged medically unfit on 1 December 1912. He later served in the 1st Rhodesia Regiment from 22 December 1914 to 16 July 1915 and the B.S.A.P. Service Company from 13 October 1915 to 10 April 1916, when he was again discharged unfit.

When an editor was needed for the embryo Regimental Magazine in March 1911, he was called for and given the task, as it was known that he had experience in this field. He had previously been employed as a journalist in the Press Gallery of the House of Commons and had contributed articles and cartoons to various national newspapers in London. He continued as the editor for one year when he was struck down with enteric fever and after a long illness was discharged. He returned to Rhodesia as a civilian and edited the *Rhodesian Journal* and worked also as the assistant editor of the *Rhodesian Annual* and *Rhodesia Seen From Within*.

When Moore-Richie left on his appointment as editor of *Nongai* in South Africa, he returned and edited the *Police Review* again up until the outbreak of war in 1914. It is believed that he returned to the United Kingdom after his discharge and eventually went abroad again. He had a brother, Phillip, also a journalist, who was the war correspondent for the *Westminster Gazette* during the Balkan Wars of 1912. Phillip had contributed material to the *Police Review* under the pen name of 'Fil'. His younger brother, 2nd Lieutenant C.I.V. Bussy, South Staffordshire Regiment was killed in action on 3 February 1916 and his older brother, 2nd Lieutenant J.H. Bussy, also of the Staffordshires, was killed in action on 28 September 1916, also in France.

Wilfred Bussy married Miriam Deacon at Battle, Sussex, in the third quarter of 1925, and died at Rangoon a year later, on 4 August 1926. A Reuters Telegram in *The Times* of 5 August 1926 reads: 'The death is announced of Mr W. Bussy, assistant editor of the *Rangoon Times.*' He was only forty-four years old.

The story of the Author's death in Rangoon is supported by the fact that the BT27 Series at the National Archives show that Wilfred Bernard Bussy sailed as a passenger in the Japanese ship S.S. *Hirano Maru* from London to Singapore via Durban on 27 July 1917. He listed his age as 32 years, profession Journalist and stated that he intended to reside in the Malay States.

(Reason for discrepancies in ages not known. Some of the biographical information supplied by Mike Bussy, Port Moresby, PNG, 2009)

Note by Cliff Rogers

The History by Trooper Bussy was first published in a series of articles in the *Police Review*, the then magazine of the British South Africa Police, up to August 1914.

It was the practice of the author to put a short note at the end of each chapter outlining the content of the following one. After the last article he wrote; 'To be continued. Chapter VIII will describe in full the siege at Elands River'. This was the August 1914 issue of the *Police Review* and I have not been able to find any evidence that further copies of the *Police Review* were ever printed. The *Rhodesia Defence Force Journal* was first printed in November 1914 and they did not continue the B.S.A.P. History Series. With the outbreak of war on the 4th August 1914, this would be understandable.

Note by Wilfred Bussy
at the start of the serialisation of his History

On another page we have set down our first instalment of the promised history of the Police.

The task of writing it has been even a more difficult one than we anticipated.

  The information concerning the early days of the corps which we have gleaned has been of the scantiest, and we must once more appeal to our older hands and to the numerous Rhodesians who have served in the Regiment for help. Any little notes and reminiscences that deal with our story will be most welcome – the lighter the better, as we hope to keep the narrative as distinct from the conventional "dry-as-dust" history as possible. We shall be especially grateful for any sketches and photographs that have survived the early days, and we promise to take every care of any pictures we may receive, returning them on the completion of their reproduction with our warmest thanks for the loan. To the handful of veterans who are still in the corps we make yet one more appeal and hope that this time we are making it loud enough to reach them.

W.B.B.

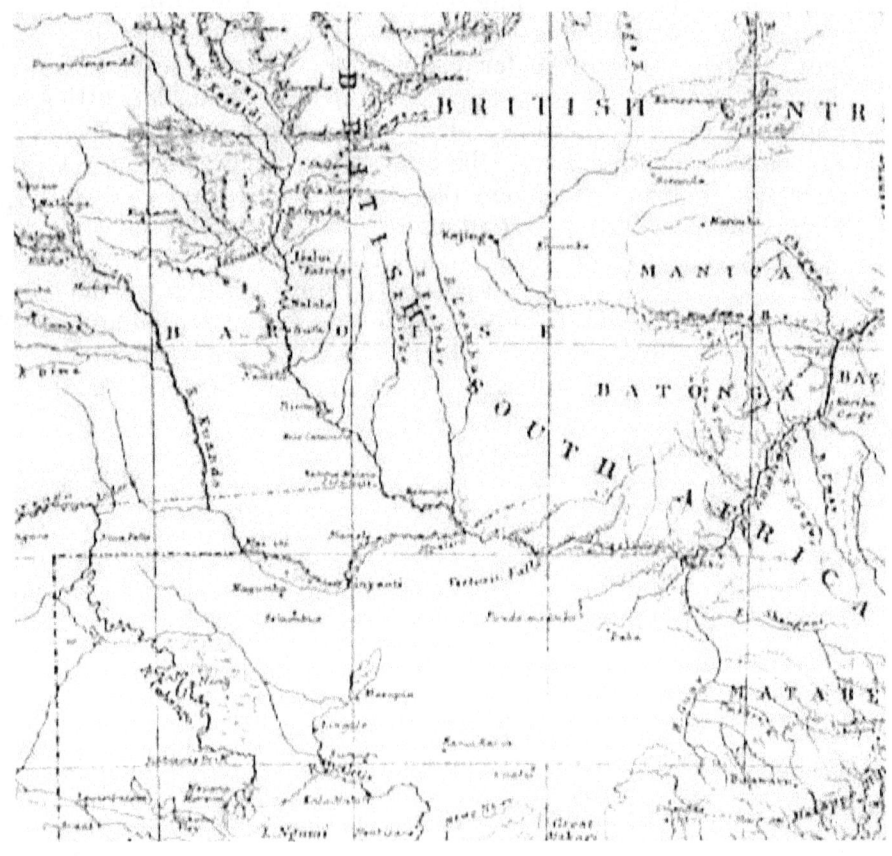

CHAPTER ONE

Introduction: The Birth of the B.B.P.

South African patriotism is a curious thing. In no part of the world is the quality so unattended by a knowledge of local history. The citizens and warriors of the sub-continent seem to need none of the pride which is begotten by the memory of great deeds and gallant ventures; yet they have always been readier than any to give all that lay in their power to give in the service of their country without reward, usually without the hope of fame, and frequently in face of almost certain failure. The records of the newer countries of Africa are meagre and usually incorrect, while stories of the regiments that did more than anything to take and to make them are so shrouded in mystery that, were it not for the infrequent oases of that literary desert, the Government *Blue Book*, it would be well nigh impossible for any one to write such a history as that we are now attempting, and to tell the story of the British South Africa Police in a manner worthy of a mounted police corps, which, though young in years, has proved itself to be second to none, so far as achievement and ability are concerned.

Perhaps, the ignorance of their own past prevailing even amongst the veterans in the Police is to be explained by the fact that the regiment has not always existed as one composite whole. The history of the B.S.A.P. is really the story of five brave corps, and it will be our task to give in brief a description and a short history of each in turn, showing how one was a necessary forerunner of the next, until there came a time for their amalgamation into the body as we know it to-day.

The earliest of the five corps we have mentioned was the Bechuanaland Border Police, founded on the conclusion of Warren's expedition of December '84, with the object of acting as a frontier guard, preventing Boer aggression in Bechuanaland, and keeping the road to the North. In 1889, on the granting of the Charter to the B.S.A. Co., authority was given to the Company (in Clause 10), to raise and equip a police force of its own, and the B.S.A.Co.'s Police came into being, the original members having transferred from the B.B.P. After the first Matabele Rebellion it was seen that, to stay the hand of insurrection and crime, that was only too likely to be raised at any time by the embittered native population, it was necessary to increase the standing force, and to build up a mounted constabulary that would be capable of looking after the interests of both the white and black, checking disorder, and acting, if called upon, as a military body as well. Such a force was raised under the distinct titles of the Mashonaland Mounted Police and the Matabeleland Mounted Police, one force in cohesion, discipline and similarity of training, while the local administration was peculiar to either division. These two corps, together with the B.B.P., were amalgamated on October 8th 1896, and from that date the B.S.A.P., in which we serve today, has flourished, always developing and attaining greater efficiency with each year of its history, until it has come to be coupled throughout Great Britain and the Empire with one other corps, the North-Western Police of Canada as a type of everything that a good Colonial police force should be.

Enrolment for the Bechuanaland Border Police began at Barkly West on the 15th of August 1885. The recruits had all either served in the Bechuanaland Field Force or some Colonial corps, and nearly all were known either to Colonel Frederick Carrington, who assumed command, or his officers. By the 28th August, the force was completely organised and equipped, and in a position to allow of the immediate withdrawal from the country of all other troops.

The strength of the corps in non-commissioned officers and men was 477. The original strength in riding animals was 453, this number being taken over from the Bechuanaland Field Force and the Bechuanaland Mounted Police, but at the end of the first year of the new regiment it was recorded that over one-sixth had died from horse sickness and other diseases, which were to prove the greatest hindrance to effective transport and travel that this part of the world was to know. The force was well provided with artillery and the means of transport, and was trained from the start to be equally viable as irregular cavalry, mounted infantry, or ordinary police. It was their task to guard a line of frontier extending for over 400 miles. They had many extraordinary duties, such as conducting diplomatic relations, and settling long-standing disputes between rival native chiefs, maintaining postal communication throughout the country, and guarding all waters and pumps at the several watering places. The bases of occupation were Taungs, Vryburg and Mafeking, a complete troop being stationed at each of the former stations, the remainder of the corps being at Mafeking. Other places in the country and along the Transvaal Border were garrisoned as occasion required. A well known officer has left us a vivid picture of the personnel of those early days:

> They are as fine a set of fellows as I have ever worked with, men that you could go anywhere and do anything with. They are all hard seasoned men in the pride of manhood, most of them are Africanders, that they have lived in the open veldt all their lives, who can shoot straight; ride well and keep their wits about them. What more could the most fastidious commander require. Men in whom I place the utmost reliance, and upon whom I could depend to get me out of a nasty corner should it ever be my fate to drop into one. Among them is a slight sprinkling only of youngsters fresh from Home, but they are quite lost among the seasoned old hands. In any case they are of the right sort, and as full of grit and dash as the men who rushed Quebec at the point of the bayonet, and carried San Sebastian by storm.
>
> Their physique is magnificent, and if the shade of the great and departed Frederick could but see them, through the medium of a kindly Mahatma, he, or I suppose I ought to say it, would go into raptures over them. It is not so much their height, though they are almost giants, but the excellence of their proportions and condition, and the display of muscle and sinew, which is simply superb. A troop of gladiators, a glimpse at whose martial bearing and dare-devil appearance would have gladdened the eyes and heart of Imperial Rome.
>
> But, unfortunately, as mounted infantry they are too tall and too heavy, and whoever enlisted them as such is much to blame. I believe Carrington is the responsible party, as he raised the corps, though I expect he had little or no choice in the matter, and had to take all the men he could get.
>
> The majority of my men, as I said before, have led an outdoor life, and are prospectors, farmers and miners: but

of course trades of all sorts are represented, and were we to start a Utopia of our own, the community would be self supporting (a remark which has often been justly made on our present day police.-*W.B.*), with professors to instruct us, not only in the highest mental culture, but in the art called culinary; while to clothe mind and body we have tailors with sporting instincts and fighting proclivities.

Many of them are Colonials, born of English, Scotch and Irish parents, who came out and settled, some thirty or forty years ago, in Natal and the Cape; and some few are men who came out as youngsters on their own hook. A goodly number are of Dutch and Huguenot (French) descent; and the minority are recent arrivals from England and America, one man a very fine specimen, too, hailing from the far off city of the Golden Gate.

A mixed lot, you will say, but a splendid mixture, I can tell you in earnest, in a small way, of what Great Britain might do, if Imperial federation were an accomplished fact. Don't think me too enthusiastic, for I mean what I say. Only imagine what a hotch-potch of humanity it is, and how Dickens and Thackeray would have revelled in the varied types, with their different peccadilloes and idiosyncrasies. Scotch caution and prudence, English sangfroid and doggedness, Irish geniality and impulse, Dutch phlegm and conservatism, French verve and excitability.

Such were the men and, as for their achievements, they did all that was asked of them, and it was by means of their lonely patrols that the peace was kept in one of the most difficult savage countries in the world. Of incident, as statesmen use the word, they saw but little. Now and again rumours would reach them of filibustering expeditions from the Dutch side, but nothing came of them, if indeed they were not all creations of more imagination than wisdom. No sounds of war came to break the peaceful monotony of their daily labours, but the first happening to stir the regiment and even to threaten the corps as a whole was purely of social import as we shall show.

CHAPTER TWO

The Charges of the Wesleyan Missionary Society – An Early Patrol Report

Before the formation of the B.B.P., practically the only white men in Bechuanaland to exercise any permanent personal authority over the natives of the country consisted of a small band of Missionaries, prominent among whom were the ministers of the Wesleyan Missionary Society. These gentlemen, undoubtedly, felt most keenly the loss of prestige which naturally followed on the arrival of a strong official element in what they considered to be their own hunting grounds. Bitterness was shown in many ways. It was hinted that the authorities were incapable of administrating the country in a fit and peaceable manner, and finally, the many insinuations that had been thrown out in both the Colony and the Home country, culminated in a most violent written attack on the B.B.P. by one Watkins, a Wesleyan minister. His chief charges were to the effect that drunkenness and immorality were rampant among the troops in Mafeking, that the canteens were conducted in a disorderly manner, that there had come to his knowledge cases of the raping of Baralong women by the troopers, and that the Sabbath was consistently broken by the men of the regiment.

Although there was no substantial foundation whatsoever for these charges, and regardless of the fact that Mr. Watkins had only been in Mafeking a few days, and admitted that he had not himself the evidence of personal observation, the Wesleyan Missionary Society hastened to endorse his action. The Colonial Office at once took the matter up, and an exhaustive enquiry was made. Meanwhile, the Rev. J. Harris, the Church of England minister at Mafeking, Acting Chaplain to the regiment, gallantly threw himself into the breach, and expressed his complete disapproval of an agitation calculated to arouse and accentuate an embittered feeling between the natives and the English, and to make the former more discontented with the beneficent government provided for them to some extent by the latter.

As acting chaplain he wished to indignantly deny that the men of the B.B. Force in Mafeking Camp were the drunken and lewd set which they had been made out to be.

'I have seen surprisingly little drunkenness either in the camp or in the town, and the men as a rule behave in as decorous and seemly a manner as could the memorialists themselves. What I am concerned to do is to state my own deliberate opinion and conviction that such rumours do not represent the true state of affairs, but are, probably, ignorantly or unwittingly, a gross exaggeration or a serious perversion of the facts known to all those who can speak from experience, and not from hearsay alone.'

Similar testimony was brought forward by the leading civil and military authorities of the country, and in the end it was proved that the principal charges, those of rape, were founded on incidents which had occurred before the B.B.P. had come into existence, while Mr. Watkin's remaining accusations were proved to have no foundation.

A public indignation meeting was held in the Mafeking Assembly Rooms on January 12th 1887, and no less than 107 persons were present, including Mr. Appelbe (Wesleyan Missionary Society), Mr. Harris and Father McCabe, the Catholic minister. Resolutions to the effect that the Society's charges were absolutely without foundation were carried by acclamation, only one person besides Mr. Appelbe voting against them. Such was the end of the most menacing social crisis that has ever threatened the corps throughout its history, killing the unwarranted charges that, had they been successful, might have changed the whole character and practically the whole personnel of the regiment for they had been noised abroad throughout England and the Empire, as well as in the country of their origin.

It is pleasant to be able to turn from an unsavoury chronicle like that we have just completed to a slight picture of the actual police work of the new regiment. It is recorded in the patrol report of Lieut. and Adjutant Bethell, dated August 31st 1886, and deals with a journey of 381 miles undertaken by the Lieut. and a trooper, Ayton. Reading the original report, one is tempted to wonder how long a period of training would be required by the modern recruit before becoming fit to perform the exploits of the old time Colonial corps. Nowadays there are troopers who will grumble at the deprivation of their jam for a few days, but the time of which we write was an heroic age, and the men, being, of necessity, removed from practically every luxury, did men's work as by force of habit, conscious only of the fact that they were doing but their duty.

Lieut. Bethell's patrol started from the Nata on June 17th for the Zambesi. He and his companion rode horses, and were accompanied by a pack horse which carried a total weight under 100lbs., including the pack-saddle. And this for a journey into a district which contained one permanent white resident for the whole 381 miles. The pack consisted of 10lbs. of meal, 5lbs. of biscuits, 4lbs. biltong, some coffee and cocoa and the blankets. On the second day out the bag of meal was left by the wayside as a reserve for the return journey to Mafeking.

From the 21st the two travellers had the misfortune to trek through waterless country for two days and, taking with them a handful of biscuits and a tin of cocoa, were obliged to leave their exhausted pack-horse and explore for some likely vlei. When they did find what they sought at Deka, they discovered that they were a good 30 miles away from their pack, and of course had to return.

On the 25th the patrol. reached Pendamatenga where the horses proved to be too exhausted to proceed further. From this place they decided to walk and leaving the animals, made for the Zambesi and the Falls, returning to their starting point on July 7th, thus having walked 200 miles in 13 days, or an average of 14 miles a day through the wildest bush and scrub country, plentifully sprinkled with the formidable granite kopjes that one meets with so often to the south of the Zambesi Valley, and frequently changing to those long, bewildering stretches of hot, loose sand.

On arriving once more at the place where they had left the reserve rations, it was found that Kaffirs had removed them. Shortly after, Tpr. Ayton's horse became once more disabled for the time being. The pack was found next day untouched, but the other saddle horse was seen to be done up and the two men started cheerfully on another walking stretch of 300 miles to Shoshong, most of which was through very heavy sand. For most of this journey they were without the materials for making bread. Meat they hoped to shoot along the road but found nothing with the exception of a few pheasants. On July 12th, at the beginning of some 45 miles of waterless country, the third horse proved to be knocked up. Later, they had to negotiate another 100 miles of dry country, when all their food consisted of a few little sand grouse, and after a last seven days of cart travel arrived in Shoshong, where the trooper remained. On August 10th, Lieut. Bethell went on to Mafeking.

But these journeys of exploration performed by the men of the early police required erudition as well as pluck, if they were to be carried out successfully. Thus we find Lieut. Bethel reporting most vividly and accurately on the soils of the districts passed through, their flora and fauna, even to an almost exhaustive list of the birds, beetles and butterflies, and the changing climate of the country. He describes the manners and customs of the natives met with, their physique and character. We find in the narrative most useful hints as to the locality and habits of the tse tse fly and other poisonous creatures; besides well considered notes on the tropical diseases and their remedies, with his own observations thereon. To the report was attached an excellently drawn road report, or map, of the patrol.

And all this formed only one small portion of the Police work of those early days. If the achievements of the old B.B.P. are ever told in full, as they should be, they will provide a tale indeed which should be treasured in the memory as long as there is a white man left in South Africa to recall them. And when we speak proudly of our great regiment of to-day, it should never be forgotten that, but for those gallant pioneers of the B.B.P., the British South Africa Police might have turned out very differently in the making.

CHAPTER THREE

Tribal Wars – the Grobelaar Case
– The Formation of the Company's Police

One of the most fascinating phases of the history of the old B.B.P. is that which deals with their work as arbitrators and peacemakers between the various native tribes in Bechuanaland. As we have pointed out, the strength of the regiment was not numerically great, and had the responsible members of the force failed at all in the use of their tact and discretion, when dealing with the frequent native feuds, it is possible that the country might have been plunged into an inferno of strife and bloodshed from which it would have taken her many years to emerge. But the officers and men of the B.B.P. had deleted the word failure from their vocabulary and, acting always on the impulse of their instinct of fair-play tempered by a firm hand, they succeeded in training the native mind to the discipline of peaceful citizenship that the native of Bechuanaland shows to-day.

Perhaps the principal tribal feud to be recorded in that part of the world, since the British occupation, came to a head in May 1887. The Baselika, under Kobe, one of the oldest chiefs in the country, had come into collision with some of Khama's people, the Mangwato, firing on the latter and killing two of the tribesmen, one of them being Sipae, a cousin of Khama. Kobe and Selika, his son, at once began to mass their followers and prepare for war. Orders were given that the Mangwato were to be shot on sight and, to complicate matters, Grobelaar, a Dutchman who was afterwards to give considerable trouble to the British authorities, had arrived on the Transvaal side of the Crocodile River with two wagons and proceeded to sell rifles and ammunition to the Baselika.

On May 16th, Khama, with an army of 4,000 warriors, left Shoshong for Nwapa, the mountain stronghold of Kobe's people. The force was accompanied by Lieut. Bates and 28 men of the B.B.P. whose duty it was to see that the fighting was kept within proper limits and that Khama's troops did not exceed their functions as a punitive expedition. On arrival at Nwapa, Lieut. Bates despatched a messenger to Kobe, suggesting that a time and place should be appointed so that the two chiefs might meet and come to terms without further bloodshed. The message was ignored. On the following day another was sent, demanding an answer before sundown, and adding a threat that, if the demand was not complied with, Lieut. Bates would stand aside and leave a free hand to Khama. This note had some effect. A native from the Baselika returned with the messenger under a flag of truce. He carried a despatch from Selika, who stated that if the Mangwato would turn and go back to their homes, he would see that his father's people did likewise. Lieut. Bates replied that he insisted on either Kobe or Selika coming over in person before sundown, otherwise the attack would commence without fail. As the officer explained later, in his report on the affair, a further delay was impossible, as he knew that the Baselika had sent for and expected assistance, while the horses and oxen belonging both to Khama and the B.B.P. had been without water for 48 hours.

At 8.30 on the following morning permission was given to Khama to advance to the attack, whereupon the Mangwato started to carry the mountain on which the Baselika were posted, converging on three different points. A brisk battle was soon in progress, and after two hours' keen fighting the mountain was cleared. Khama lost seven men killed and eight wounded while the dead bodies of thirteen of the Baselika were afterwards found on the field.

Khama at once sent for Selika, but he had disappeared. The former then met Kobe, who declared that the fighting had not been undertaken at his desire, but at the instigation of the young firebrand Selika. Khama replied that the Baselika could go where they wished in future, but they were not to stay in the country. He further gave Kobe a good wagon as a token of his personal esteem and, peace being declared, returned to Shoshong with his army. Lieut. Bates was highly complimented by the authorities on the action he had taken and shortly afterwards received his captaincy.

Meanwhile, and, in fact, ever since the formation of the B.B.P., rumours had been coming through from the Transvaal, dealing with proposed Boer treks and filibustering expeditions to the North. Undoubtedly the authorities in Pretoria had some idea of one day acquiring the rich new countries, more especially that one which was ruled by Lo Bengula, and which had been reported on so favourably by the early explorers, British and Boer. It is quite possible that many of the projected raids, which for some reason had never yet taken actual form, were planned by the wily old President himself, but naturally he was careful to disavow all connection with any conspiracies that might have been hatched. At last one of these ventures took practical shape and resulted in the affair that we now know as the Grobelaar Case. For some time the natives of Bechuanaland had reported that bands of Dutchmen were gathering on the border and seemed to be making ready for a march to the North. They were well armed and provisioned. One of these bands finally came to blows with some of Khama's people a few miles from Macloutsie, and well on the Protectorate ground. The Dutch leader, Grobelaar, was proved afterwards to have been responsible for the attack, and besides counting many Dutch and British in his following, he was escorted by thirty regular Boer artillerymen. The result of the encounter was that Grobelaar was killed and his raid frustrated at the onset. The affair created an enormous stir in the Transvaal, and at one time it even looked as though war between the British and Dutch was inevitable. Grobelaar was spoken of in official despatches as Consul-General, and the British authorities were informed that he had been on his way to Bulawayo at the time the incident took place, as Boer Consul in Lo Bengula's territories. However, Matabeleland formed part of the British sphere of influence, and no sanction for Grobelaar's assumption of this office had been granted by our authorities, while Lo Bengula himself denied the truth of the Dutch version entirely.

A commission was formed to enquire into the case, and for a time the matter dropped. But bitter feeling between the two white races was all the time becoming more pronounced, trouble was expected at any moment, and meanwhile the little handful of B.B.P., the only defence force in the country, was being worked to a degree that probably no Police force has ever exceeded. Finally, it was seen that to safeguard the Protectorate and to look after the new territories that were being acquired in the North, it was necessary to raise the strength of the corps, which at that time was only 150 strong, and 200 men were added to the Regiment.

Shortly after this, Rhodesian history really commences, and is to be seen at its most critical stage. The Charter had been granted, but it was obvious that without some well defined show of strength any sort of occupation in Matabeleland would be disputed by the Dutch, as well as by the younger and more fiery spirits among Lo Ben's own warriors. Hence it became essential to raise a corps of some sort under the authority of the new Company and, with the experienced aid of Sir Frederick Carrington, the B.S.A. Co.'s Police were formed. The B.B.P. were reduced to 200 men and the Company's Police quickly grew to five troops, under Lieut.-Colonel Pennefather (of the Inniskilling Dragoons). In training, the B.S.A.C.P. were assimilated to the B.B.P. from the start, and for the best part of their horses and stores they looked to the sister regiment, besides taking most of the retrenched B.B.P. into their own ranks. Headquarters were formed at Macloutsie, close to the B.B.P. camp, where the new regiment was to wait a while until such time as they should be judged thoroughly efficient and in every way fit for the strenuous days that lay before them. A fort capable of holding 200 men was built by the men of both corps, between the two camps. Against artillery or Dutch rifle fire it would have proved practically useless, as it was commanded from the North and East by higher ground, but it was strong enough to resist any attack the natives were capable of. Its greatest defect was want of water, which lay over a half-mile away.

Recruits' course became brisk and wearisome for the whole corps, but there were welcome periods of diversion. Fishing and shooting of the best were to be had in the neighbourhood, matches of football and cricket were arranged between the various troops and the two regiments, and there were the wildest of the remounts to be broken in. There was leg pulling galore, as was to be expected from a body of men so cosmopolitan in type as the pioneer police, but always in the background there lurked that grim spirit of endeavour and determination that have always characterised the early Rhodesian, whether as policeman or civilian.

CHAPTER FOUR

Great Trek – Builders of Empire – the Occupation of Mashonaland

The start of the Company's Police on the Great Trek which was to result in the occupation of Rhodesia and the founding of the Capital, was delayed by the inexperience of the Pioneers who were to march with them. These formed a corps 180 strong, which had been raised by Major Frank Johnson at Kimberley. The men were of the sturdiest type, similar to their comrades of the B.S.A.C.P, and their column was composed chiefly of Britishers and British Afrikanders. They were divided into three troops, the first two of which were mounted infantry, while the third formed the artillery troop, their guns consisting of a 7-pounder and quick-firing Maxims. To this troop was attached a detail of bluejackets to handle the quick-firing guns. The Pioneer Corps joined their comrades at Macloutsie, on June 13th 1890, and drilling at once became more severe than ever for the whole army, more especially as the attitude of Lo Bengula and his impis was getting less friendly every day, and it was thought by the authorities that an attack on the column was inevitable when once the king's territories in Matabeleland had been entered.

Towards the end of June, Major-General Lord Methuen, the Adjutant General of the British Forces in South Africa, arrived at Macloutsie. He proceeded to inspect both the Pioneers and the Police, with a view to testing their fitness to proceed. Two reviews were held, and one of them consisted of a sham fight between the B.S.A.C.P. and the B.B.P. Everything went off without a hitch, and the General expressed himself as entirely satisfied with the aptitude for their work which the men had shown, congratulated the column and bade them god-speed.

Finally, a move was made. One troop of Police was left behind to garrison Macloutsie, while a second stayed at Tuli, on the Southern boundary line of Matabeleland, which was reached on July 1st. The other three troops, 'A' under Major Heany, 'B' under Capt. Hoste, and 'C' under Capt. Borrow, pushed forward with the column, which now numbered 480 men. Col. Pennefather was in supreme command, Mr. F.C. Selous, the famous hunter, being his guide and intelligence officer. Two hundred of Khama's picked warriors marched with the little force, and they were to prove invaluable, as upon crossing the border, after receiving a warning message from the king, all the other natives attached to the column as drivers and leaders cleared from the Expedition. As Mr. Selous stated in his book:

'Great numbers deserted, and it is my belief that, had not Khama come to our assistance at this juncture, not a coloured boy would have crossed the Tuli, and the expedition in that case would have been most lamentably crippled.'

The column left Tuli on July 6th. Every precaution was taken against attack. On a halt being made, a laager was formed, the 65 wagons being disposed in a diamond-shaped wedge, with either a 7-pounder or a Maxim at each corner. Each wagon had its fixed place in the formation, and every man knew his exact position, so that the laager could be built up almost on the instant the presence of a hostile body was suspected. On the march, the wagon train was preceded by a strong advance guard which rode some 200 yards ahead. On either side of the wagons rode troopers in pairs at a distance of about 200 yards from each other, while the rear was defended by a guard similar to the one in front. Police scouts were thrown out in all directions to examine the country round, and ensure that no surprise attack was made on the column. As another precautionary measure an electric searchlight was carried, this being supplied by a dynamo run by the steamengine of a contemplated sawmill.

Thus commenced one of the finest marches in all history, a march of less than 500 venturesome Britishers through 400 miles of trackless desert infested by hostile savages, and marked at every stage by drifts, barred by great rocks; mountain walls, through which a practicable road had to be cut, long torturing stretches of country that held no water; or well nigh impenetrable bushveld. Such an undertaking had to be carried out before the object of the expedition could be achieved, the occupation of Mashonaland and the establishment of Rhodesia as yet another unit in the proud possessions of the British Empire.

Horse-sickness set in to add to the inconveniences of the work, but the greatest difficulty of all proved to be the actual making of the road.

Throughout its course dense forests had to be attacked, the trees hewn down and the undergrowth cleared away, the sandy stretches that lay alongside the rivers had to be hardened with lengths of 'corduroy' for the passage of heavily laden wagons, and in the dry river beds enormous boulders had to be moved bodily aside. The work was allotted to two troops, and each troop was divided into two sections. Half the men worked at a time while the other half followed with their horses, so that the whole party would be ready at a moment's notice in case of any sudden attack. The makers of the road kept always about ten miles in advance of the main body.

The long expected attack never came, although Lo Bengula himself had tried to scare the column with a threat to let loose his impis. But this was probably nothing more than sheer bluff, as a considerable force of the B.B.P. had been moved up to the Western boundary of Matabeleland, and the king must have seen that any attack on the column would have resulted in his warriors being 'sandwiched' between the two white forces, with disastrous consequences to themselves. However, the expedition was not allowed to proceed without opposition of some sort.

Lo Bengula, knowing that the expedition could not now be stayed, and fearing trouble from the presence of so many white men in his country, besides probably regretting that he ever consented to the granting of the Charter, had demanded that the column should make its way through Bulawayo, so that he could see for himself the nature of the force. To this effect he sent a message by Mr. Colenbrander, the hunter, to Col. Pennefather, which contained the menace, 'Who are you, and where are you going? What do you want, and by whose orders are you here? Whither are you leading your young men, like so many sheep? Do you think they will ever return. Go back, or I will not be responsible for the consequences, white blood can flow as well as black.' To this threat Col. Pennefather replied: 'I am an officer of the Queen of England, and my orders are to go to Mashonaland, and there I am going. We do not want to fight, we only want to dig for gold, and are taking this road to avoid your young men; but if they attack us, we know how to defend ourselves.'

As a result of the King's warning, anxiety was shown by the leaders of the expedition to win through the thick bushveld to the highlands before the messengers could regain Bulawayo, and an impi be sent to stop the advance. The scouts, after a great deal of work, found a practicable opening in the hills, which they called 'Providential Pass,' and the uplands near Fort Victoria were reached by the main body on August 13th. Here Mr. Colenbrander arrived with a further message to the effect that the impis had defied the King and were fully determined to slay every white man in the column, and further, that 9,000 warriors were actually on their way to carry out this intention. Col. Pennefather's sole answer to this was an order that the advance should continue. Fresh scouts were sent out to scour the district and look for signs of the Matabele. Some of them returned with the information that a large impi was encamped on the banks of a river which lay across the column's line of route to their front. The expedition continued to push forward, and no signs of the Matabele were seen by the main body, though it was evident that they were trekking parallel to the column.

Henceforth the difficulties were practically at an end, and the column was neither attacked nor unduly hindered. Midway between Fort Victoria and Mount Hampden another fort was built, it was christened Fort Charter, and on September 10th, less than four months after the Pioneers had quitted Mafeking, a journey of 800 miles had been performed, a practicable road had been cut for 400 miles; three forts had been erected for the protection of later travellers; and the gallant little band of adventurers had shown the world that the Empire still had something extraordinary in the way of courage and enterprise to boast of. Indeed, there has been nothing finer in the annals of any country than the tale of the great trek that made Rhodesia.

On September 11th 1890, the first and last ceremonial parade of the Pioneer Column was held at Mount Hampden or as it came to be called, Fort Salisbury. The Union Jack was run up in the centre of the saluting troops, prayer was offered up by the Rev. Canon Balfour, and, amid cheers for the Queen, a salute of 21 guns was fired by the 7-pounder battery. So was the country formally taken possession of in the name of Her Majesty, and another stone was added to the foundations of that mighty Empire, that surely can never die while her sons are of the stamp of the men that made Rhodesia.

CHAPTER FIVE

An Insult to the Flag – War with the Portuguese
– The Amazing Seven – The Victory at Massi-Kessi
– The Acquisition of Manicaland

The pioneer Column remained as one force until October 1st 1890 when Fort Salisbury was built and the volunteers disbanded. Round the police camp there rapidly sprang up a collection of rough and ready shanties that were to form the nucleus for the town of Salisbury. Many of the inhabitants were not slow to lose the eager spirit of hopefulness which had accompanied the march of the pioneers, for the fortunes they had thought to find in the fruitful goldfields of Mashonaland proved to be less plentiful than they had anticipated and a host of disenchanted adventurers were using the town merely as a breathing place whence they were to make the return journey to the South. At the same time further expeditions of civilians were following hard on the track of the pioneers. Then the rains came on. Scores of wayfarers died, having been held up by the swollen rivers, horsesickness and the ravages of tse tse fly, and detained without medicine, and without food, on the fever-stricken banks; famine prevailed in Salisbury itself, and, a drop in the cup of disappointment, it was found that the projected road of communication between the town and the East Coast was not practicable as it would have run through a belt of tse tse-fly country which cattle would have been unable to cross. Altogether the fortunes of the new country did not look bright at all in the early days, and, had not the original settlers being of the sturdy undaunted type that had accomplished the trek from the South, the Rhodesia of today would never have been accomplished at all.

Perhaps, the police at that time suffered less than the rest of the population, for at least they with the Administrator could boast buildings of a substantial nature for their dwelling places, while the mining camp around them was a mere collection of shaky huts. But the troopers were to prove themselves none the less hardy on that account, and, no later than the early days of

'91 they were to succeed in as gallant an enterprise that had ever been achieved, and set all England and the Empire ringing with praise of their gallantry.

On quitting the Pioneer Column at the end of the previous August, Mr. Selous had hastened to Manicaland, a noble piece of territory which lay in the highlands to the south-east of Salisbury. The country, which was well suited for European colonisation, was under the rule of a native named Umtassa, from whom Selous, together with Dr. Jameson and Mr. Colquhoun, the Administrator, succeeded in obtaining a concession of mineral rights on behalf of the Chartered Company. But the Portuguese of the East Coast had already greeted with much disfavour the incursion of Britishers into Mashonaland, and had decided that the sphere of British influence in that direction was to extend no further. Accordingly they claimed as their own property the whole territory of Manicaland and announced their intention of taking decisive action against any of the British South Africa Company's forces that might see fit to enter it. Two Portuguese officers, Colonels Paiva d'Andrada and Gouveia, followed this intimation with a show of armed strength, and marched into the country at the head of some 300 native troops, with the object of forcing Umtassa to withhold his concession to the British. The band halted at Massi-Kessi, a small fort on the eastern frontier which contained a small British garrison. The Britishers were compelled to retreat, while the Union Jack was hauled down and trampled underfoot by the excited Portuguese. The news caused a howl of resentment to circulate throughout the Empire, and a European war might have resulted, had not the little handful that formed the population of the new colony been quite confident in their strength to right the affair in a satisfactory manner.

A little army of about thirty of the B.S.A. Co's Police under Major Forbes, was despatched to Umtassa's kraal. They found the Portuguese force had arrived before them, but Major Forbes, acting on the impulse of an almost unparalleled 'cheek,' arrested the two officers in front of their own troops, and sent them to Salisbury under a strong escort, he disarmed the soldiers and expelled them from Manicaland. Not content with this, he pushed into Massi-Kessi and recaptured the fort. Finally, although his force was hardly sufficient to act as a satisfactory garrison for Massi-Kessi, he conceived the well nigh inconceivable idea of capturing Beira, the Portuguese capital. The whole army at his disposal now numbered but six troopers! Picture seven stolid Englishmen, either possessing not one grain of the sense of humour, or marching like the heroes of Dumas, with tongues in their cheeks the whole while quietly setting out to achieve a feat every bit as absurd as Don Quixote's charge on the windmills; only difference being that these adventurers had a certain method in their madness, for it is quite possible that the sheer audacity of the idea would have pulled them through to final victory.

They did succeed in marching through an unknown country for 150 miles to the Pungwe river, where they embarked in canoes for Beira, which was efficiently garrisoned by the white troops of the Portuguese. Now, however, the Government, seeing complications ahead, interfered, and ordered Major Forbes to return to Salisbury immediately, a command which of course he had to obey.

Negotiations followed between the Company and the Portuguese authorities, and, as a result, the captured officers were permitted to return to Portuguese territory, while the Company held the lands conceded by Umtassa. Massi-Kessi reverted to Portugal. The Portuguese, however, had been made the laughing stock of the whole world, and, in spite of the terms of the settlement, they proceeded to equip a large force which was to expel the British from Manicaland and satisfy their craving for revenge. At the same time a counter force was raised in Salisbury. Several civilians rushed to volunteer, and, at length, Captain Heyman, with fifty policemen and volunteers and a 7-pounder, were despatched to Manicaland to watch the movements of a considerable Portuguese force that had collected near Massi-Kessi. The expedition halted at Chua Hill, some little distance from the Portuguese, on May 14th 1891. Opposing them lay an army of 100 whites and 400 natives, with no less than 11 quick-firing guns of the most modern description. A message was sent to Captain Heyman, assuring him if he stayed where he was any longer he would be attacked. The Englishman flatly refused to leave the place, and the assault commenced.

The British position was situated on the upper slopes of the hill, a condition that served in some degree to neutralise the enormous odds of ten to one. However, had not the Portuguese commander acted with criminal carelessness, victory must have been his. Deciding that the presence of the artillery might hamper his movements, he commanded that the guns should be left behind when his army advanced. Reaching the foot of the kopje, he commenced a hot fire on the Britishers, but the aim was bad, and the firing had but little result. Meanwhile, the Britishers reserved their fire until the enemy got well within range, and then poured volley after volley into their midst. The native levies wavered, whereupon the 7-pounder opened fire with canister, causing them to break and run like startled rabbits, not knowing what shelter to make for. The Portuguese whites still showed great gallantry, and struggled desperately to gain the hilltop, but each time they made any headway they were met by a cruel hail of bullets, and were soon forced to retreat. Captain Heyman followed up their retreat with an advance in skirmishing order across the plain, towards the fort, which at once capitulated. The British flag was hoisted and a garrison was disposed so that no counter attack could avail, while a quantity of valuable equipment, including the 11 guns, was taken possession of.

About this time, an attack was made on two boats which were proceeding up the Pungwe with stores for Sir John Willoughby, these being captured by the Portuguese and detained at Beira. Meanwhile, in Lisbon, a force of six or seven hundred men was being raised for active service, but Lord Salisbury at the Foreign Office put an end to the whole trouble by means of a strongly worded ultimatum to the Portuguese Government which had the desired effect. A treaty was concluded whereby the seaboard of S.E. Africa, as far as the Natal border, was left in the hands of Portugal, while the uplands, with the exception of a portion at Massi-Kessi, were ceded to the British. So the new Rhodesians found themselves doing the work that might have taken a large army, acting on conventional lines, to accomplish thoroughly; and so the new colony cemented the prestige among the British dominions that the work of the Great Trek had founded.

CHAPTER SIX

Dutch Aspirations – Letter to Lobengula
– A Frustrated Trek – Retrenchment – Lawlessness of
the Matabele – The Invasion of Mashonaland

Throughout the early days of the occupation, the British authorities had to keep a watchful and somewhat uneasy eye on the adventurers of the Dutch republics in the South. Since the time of the British reverses in '81, Boer statesmen had been dreaming of a gigantic African republic which was to stretch far North of the Zambesi. Hence the real origin of the filibustering republics of Stellaland and Goshen, and the necessity for Sir Charles Warren's expedition and the proclamation of Bechuanaland as a British protectorate.

For Bechuanaland was the high road to Zambesia, and had the Boers once won the ascendancy in Matabeleland there would have existed instead of a Transvaal shut in between the Vaal and the Limpopo, a Transvaal larger than Great Britain, France, Austria and Italy put together, bounded on the West by allied German territory and on the East by the Portuguese. An ambitious burgher might have stood on the banks of the Zambesi, gazing across the river into a country that could well have developed into a Dutch continent.

So early as '82, the actions of the British in Matabeleland had been foreseen. Mr. Selous, at that time a young man, happened to be at Lobengula's kraal in that year when a messenger from the South arrived with a letter, written in Dutch, for the King. It was dated 'Marico, S.A.R., March 9 1882,' and addressed to 'the great ruler, chief Lobengula, son of Umzilgaze, the great King of the Matabele nation.' It was worded thus, 'Now you must have heard that the English took away our country, the Transvaal or, as they say, annexed it. We then talked nicely for four years, and begged for our country. But no, when an Englishman once has your property in his hands, then he is like to an ape that has its hands full of pumpkin seeds. If you don't beat him to death, he will never let go. And thus all our nice talk for four years did not help us at all. Then, the English first found that it would be better to give us back our country. And we will now once more live in friendship with Lobengula as we lived in friendship with Umziligaze and such must be our friendship that so long as there is one Boer and one Matabele living these must remain friends'. After alluding to the time when the stink which the Englishman brought with him is blown away altogether, the document closes with the signature of, 'The Commandant-General of the S.A. Republic, for the Government and Administration, P.J. Joubert'.

Lo Ben was shrewd enough to see through this little effort in diplomacy, and the Dutch had to resort to more active courses in the attempt to carry out their policy as we have shown in the description of the Grobelaar case.

Even after the occurrence several of the inhabitants of the Transvaal had displayed a disposition to cross the Limpopo and raise a small Dutch colony in Southern Mashonaland. Mr. Rhodes spoke significantly on the subject in the course of a speech at Cape Town, when he warned President Kruger that no more republics would be permitted to be established in South Africa. Of course the President answered that he had no intention of sanctioning any such proceeding, and even affected surprise at the idea of his law abiding burghers making the attempt to cross the border.

Nevertheless the attempt was made by an organised force of Boers under Commandant Ferreira, an old campaigner who had earned the C.M.G. while fighting for the British in the Zulu war. The British authorities were ready, however. Every drift was held by the men of the B.S.A.C. Police, who were supported by a small contingent of the B.B.P. When the Boer column reached the river they were confronted by Dr. Jameson himself, at the head of a few Police troopers. The gallant doctor assured them that he was authorised to try to persuade them to go back in a peaceful manner but, failing this, he would not hesitate to shoot. The burghers, who had learnt something of the prowess of the Rhodesian police, took him at his word and deciding that discretion in this case was the better part of valour, turned back as quietly as they had come, without firing a shot. Ferreira and his secretary, Jerome, were made prisoners. That was the last occasion in which the Police, as a whole, had to confront an armed body of white men until the days of the ill fated raid in '96.

The last few months of 1891 brought great prosperity to the

country, and the authorities came to the conclusion that it was unnecessary to maintain a large standing body of Police any longer. The idea had been formed in Salisbury of raising a volunteer force in the neighbourhood for the protection of the district against Lobengula and his impis. The suggestion was acted upon, and, with the aid and sanction of the Company, the Mashonaland Horse were recruited under the popular command of Major Forbes. But the step was not welcomed very heartily by the majority of the settlers. The large portion of the police force, which had been disbanded, declared openly that the members of the Mashonaland Horse had been duped by the Company, and were expected to do for nothing what the police had been paid to do. The retrenchment also affected the commercial element of the community, for nearly all those who were discharged at once left the country and, as hitherto the police had formed a very large section of the population, trade began to decline. Those who remained settled on the Mashonaland Police Farms, good lands of 1,500 morgen which were granted to the police of 1890-92, for £3 quit rent, payable annually in advance. The most important clause in the titles of these landowners stated that there should be bona-fide and beneficial occupation of the lands, the desire of the Company being to procure an effective settlement of the country to prevent large tracts of land from being used up.

The disputes which the retrenchment caused were still in progress when interrupted by the great menace, which caused the eyes of all Rhodesia to be centred on, of the attitude of the Matabele. On the occupation of Mashonaland it had been found that the Mashona, while naturally excellent agricultural workers, were of no manner of use on the mines. Hence boys were drafted into the province from the Northern banks of the Zambesi and from Matabeleland. The Matabele soon proved to be a great source of worry, both to their employers and the Native Commissioners who had been appointed to supervise and protect them. They were most daring thieves and worse than that, for after a short time murders and attempted murders began to pour into Salisbury. To add trouble, it was found impossible to arrest the boys unless they were detected at the time the crimes took place, for they made straight for the Matabeleland border, over which the King had forbidden the whites to cross.

Furthermore these Matabele were planning a campaign of

vengeance against the lesser tribes of Mashonaland. Previous to the occupation natives of the Mashona, Makalaka and Banyai tribes had been regarded as slaves by their black conquerors. But now a challenge had come about. It was proclaimed by the white men that they had come into the country for the protection of these inferior tribes, and that they were going to prevent the Matabele from raiding them and stealing their women and cattle. As a result, the Mashonas began to show insolence on every possible occasion towards Lobengula and his impis, greatly incensing the young warriors, who had learnt to look upon these people as dogs, to be robbed and massacred at the will of the masters. The King tried so long as it was possible, to keep his regiments, well knowing that the Mashona were assured of the protection of the white men. At length however, the cravings for revenge proved too strong for him, and he allowed his impis to make for Mashonaland and inflict punishment on those tribes who had refused to pay his taxes or obey his decrees. Orders were given that the whites were not to be molested nor their belongings touched, and in July 1893, a large Matabele army crossed the border and entered Mashonaland.

CHAPTER SEVEN

Victoria Massacre – The Nonconformist Conscience again – Luke xiv-31 – The Preparations for War

Heedless of the remonstrations of the almost panic stricken whites, the impis of the Matabele made without delay for Victoria, the centre of the chief kraals of the Mashona. Here commenced indescribable scenes of horror. The inmates of the kraals, cowed and broken by long years of slavery and oppression, and almost incapable of the slightest resistance, were massacred and mutilated without pity by their more formidable foemen. Men, women and children alike fell to the assegai, quarter being given only to those who were the more favoured among the girls and young women.

It was thought that on the conclusion of this orgy of blood, a raid would be made on the small British community of the district, probably resulting in a general massacre of the white population. Messages were sent to Lobengula, demanding the recall of his impis, and the Government was called upon to take strong measures for the pacification of the country. Dr. Jameson rode to the scene of the murders in charge of a small body of the Company's police. Summoning the offending indunas to his presence, he told them boldly unless the massacres ceased on the instant that he would hang the Matabele chieftains, without any respect for any authority or rank they might hold. One or two of the smaller chiefs, less confident than their fellows, took the Administrator at his word, and withdrew together with their followers but these numbered only a few hundred men all told, but the impis as a whole continued in their mood of open defiance. Indeed, the threat was actually made that it would not be long before the whites met with the fate that had come to the unhappy Mashona.

Finally Dr. Jameson decreed that the regiments should leave before the coming of the next dawn, otherwise they would be attacked without any further show of words by the body of Police that lay in Victoria at the time. The order was greeted with derision by the greater part of the indunas, but some of them had seen the determination that lay behind the speech of the Administrator and in the end it was decided that the strength, and spirit of the white men should be tested. The main impis were withdrawn, but a small army of a few hundred warriors was left behind. At nightfall they were still engaged in their work of looting and burning the kraals of the Mashona they had slain, and a little band of police advanced under Captain Lendy. They were hailed by volleys from the Matabele whereupon they fired in return and made a general charge, putting the impi to flight. The Rhodesian Police, having always exhibited the energy and fearlessness of strong men, had to contend throughout their early days with the vindictive abuse and infamous insinuations that have come to be associated in the Old Country with the so called 'Noncomformist Conscience.' We have shown how the original B.B.P. was assailed by a campaign of calumny and malice only a few months after the birth of the regiment. Now the 'Humanitarians' saw their opportunity for further mischief, and both Dr. Jameson and Captain Lendy were hailed by certain individuals of influence in England as murderers, who had 'ruthlessly shot down the defenceless Matabele', an accusation for which there was no foundation whatsoever. These 'Little Englanders' declared that the Matabele had been butchered in most pitiless fashion, even after they had thrown down their arms and begged for mercy. (Curiously enough, the previous sufferings of the inoffensive Mashona were disregarded altogether). The facts of the matter were that the police had only fired after the native soldiers had commenced their volleys; that the indunas had had full warning of the consequences if they refused to obey the orders of the Administrator, and that there was not the slightest shred of evidence to show that quarter was not given to those that had appealed for it. But Rhodesia at the time was a young and struggling colony, and therefore an ideal mark for the aims of the 'Little England' army, which, after all, forms but a small portion of the population of the empire and, fortunately, possesses but a very tiny fraction of the influence which it fondly boasts.

As a result of the 'Lendy affair' it was seen by the settlers that it was high time steps were taken to check the actions and ambitions of the younger warriors of the Matabele. It was felt that no homestead in the country was safe so long as there were natives who were likely to show the aggressiveness and presumption that had been exhibited in the course of the Victoria massacre. Public meetings, which were held at Salisbury and Victoria, demanded an instant move on the part of the Government, failing which it was threatened that an appeal would be made to the Imperial authorities to send troops, and take over the country as a Crown Colony. The Administrator telegraphed to Mr. Rhodes at Cape Town, pointing out the state of affairs and asking for advice. He explained that the attitude of the settlers towards the Government had become really threatening, and asked if he should lead an armed force into Matabeleland and crush the power of the turbulent warriors once and for all. Mr. Rhodes at once despatched a characteristic answer in a wire which was surely one of the most laconic on record, the wording of the telegram being merely, 'Read Luke xiv, 31.' On looking up the verse indicated, Dr. Jameson read as follows:- 'Or what king, going to make war against another king sitteth not down first, and consulteth whether he is able with ten thousand to meet him coming against him with twenty thousand?' This was obviously a reference to the small number of available white troops, considerably under 1000 men, and the difficulty of contending with them against the whole might of Lobengula and the Matabele nation. However, Dr. Jameson knew the stuff of which his pioneers were made and trusted them. His answer ran, 'Have read Luke xiv, 31'. So was the fate of the Matabele decided upon, and preparations were commenced for the immediate invasion of Matabeleland, the sanction of the Imperial authorities having already been granted. The necessary funds for the campaign were provided by Mr. Rhodes himself.

 The British fighting forces were divided into four columns, which were to march on Bulawayo simultaneously. Two of these columns were in Mashonaland, the Salisbury Horse, under Major Forbes, and the Victoria Rangers, under the command of the gallant and ill-fated Major Wilson. Each column consisted of about 250 mounted infantrymen, with Maxims and other quick firing guns. A similar force was raised at Johannesburg by the Dutch Commandant Raaf. The police were well represented by 225 men of the B.B.P. with five Maxims and two 7-pounder guns under Captain Coventry. They were joined at Tuli by Commandant Raaf's force, and were accompanied further by Khama, the King of Bechuanaland, with a column of

1,800 natives. The whole force was under the command of Colonel Goold-Adams. The country to be negotiated by the B.B.P. was difficult in the extreme, and the cattle soon became exhausted with the amount of hard work that was given to them, so that progress was made but slowly and the advance guard of the Mashonaland column had already taken possession of Bulawayo while the force from Tuli lay some sixty miles from the town.

CHAPTER EIGHT

A Regrettable Incident – An 'Affair of Outposts'
– A Rear Guard Action – Arrival in Bulawayo of the
B.B.P.

Shortly after Colonel Goold-Adams and his force had quitted Tuli an unfortunate occurrence took place which was made a fresh occasion for campaigns of calumny and abuse by that section of the British press and public which was accustomed to regard Mr. Rhodes and his gallant band of followers on every possible occasion as monsters of wickedness and brutality. The real facts of the incident are as follows: Three of Lobengula's envoys arrived at the British camp at Tuli with messages for Colonel Goold-Adams, who for a time was not made aware of the reasons for their coming. Hearing from interpreters that they contemplated in fleeing from the camp, he ordered their temporary detention until he could ascertain their identity and purpose, assuring them meanwhile they had nothing to fear. The indunas, however, took fright and one of them, seizing a bayonet from a trooper, stabbed two of the guard and was shot in the attempt to escape, while a second induna, trying to get away with his comrade, met with a similar fate. The third, Inigubogubo, a half brother of Lobengula, quietly surrendered and was sent to Palapye under the charge of Mr. Dawson, the trader who had accompanied the party to the camp. As soon as the news of the affair could reach Cape Town, a searching enquiry was held by Major Sawyer, the Military Secretary to the High Commissioner and in the end Col. Goold-Adams was completely exonerated, while the Major expressed his opinion that the whole thing arose from a series of extraordinary mischances. Yet at Home, where there could be no real knowledge of what was taking place, it was openly insinuated by the 'Little England' party that the column had deliberately murdered two defenceless natives.

On the 5th October 1893, a B.B.P. patrol, consisting of a noncommissioned officer and two troopers was fired upon by about thirty Matabele, while patrolling on the south bank of the

Shashi river. The fire was returned and British reinforcements arrived, whereupon the natives retired. No casualties were reported and it is probable that the Matabele were nothing more than a chance scouting party. The Tuli Column left Macloutsie for Bulawayo on Oct. 11th. Owing to drought and the strong positions of the Matabele ahead of them, the expedition had extraordinary difficulties to contend with throughout, and the greatest caution on the part of the commander was called upon the whole way. To show clearly the scheme and progress of the march, we will annex a few extracts from the official report of the Colonel in charge.

> I started from that place (Macloutsie) with 225 officers and men, 210 horses, four Maxim guns, two seven-pounder guns, 14 wagons, and 50 native drivers. I was joined on the morning of 11th Oct. by Commandant Raaf, of the British South Africa Company, with 225 officers and men, 191 horses, one Maxim gun, and 11 wagons with their complement of drivers. I reached the Shashi River 13th Oct., and here I met the Chief Khama with 130 mounted men and between 1,700 and 1,800 dismounted men, about half of whom were armed with Martini-Henry rifles. He also had with him about 30 wagons and a number of pack oxen.
>
> The force leaving Tati numbered about 440 Europeans and about 2,000 natives, 520 horses, and about 2,000 head of oxen. The proposed route was to the Monarch Mine, thence to the Ramokabane River, up that river to its source, across to the upper waters of the Mitangwe River and along the high veldt to the eastward, striking the main road about the Fig Tree.
>
> The first move was made by sending Commandant Raaf with 100 of his mounted men and 100 of Khama's mounted men, up the main road towards Makkobis, intended as a feint to cover the flank movement to the Monarch Mine with the wagon train.
>
> The wagon train reached the Ramokabane River on 22nd and was joined as arranged by Commandant Raaf and his men on that date.
>
> So far no Matabele had actually been seen, but the spoor of their scouting parties had often been cut by ours. A party of scouts, under Mr. Selous, proceeded up the Ramokabane River to ascertain whether it was

practicable to take the column that way. He returned with the information that it was 'absolutely impossible', there being great scarcity of water, not nearly enough for our great numbers of men and animals.

I then decided to push forward on the Mpakwe River, to try to get round to the point of the hills by moving to the headwaters of the Mpakwe or Nguisi Rivers. Considering it impracticable to take the whole of my wagon teams, I pushed on with only 190 mounted men of the Bechuanaland Border Police, 200 mounted men of the British South Africa Company, 12 wagons, three Maxim guns, and two seven-pounder guns, leaving Khama and his men, and the remainder of my men in laager at the Ramokabane.

I arrived at the Siquesi River, a tributary of the Mpakwe, 29th October, without meeting with any resistance.

Here the Colonel learnt that the Matabele had visited the neighbouring kraals, raiding the cattle of the inhabitants who were Makalaka. Further, two large impis had assembled to the front of the column and it was judged wisest for the British force to go into laager and await the arrival of Khama and the men who had been left at the Ramokabane. But a junction of the main column and this rearguard was not to be effected without difficulty, for the Ramokabane party was attacked on November 1st, by a force of Matabele numbering fully 600. Captain Tancred, who was in command of the whites, lay in laager with the greater part of his troops, while the wagons, which had been delayed by the scarcity of water, were a mile and a half away. The natives attacked from of the rear of the convoy. Mounted men, led by Mr. Selous, were immediately sent out from the laager to assist in bringing in the wagons. The famous hunter arrived first on the scene of action, had already been wounded in trying to stop a rush of Matabele, when his followers came up with him. But by this time the rearmost wagon had been rushed and fired, the stores it contained had been destroyed and the oxen taken away. Mundy, a corporal, and a native driver were both assegaied. However the mounted men brought back the rest of the wagons to the shelter of the laager, where a brisk fire from the Maxims put the pursuing natives to headlong flight. The dead bodies of over 60 Matabele were counted, while the British Casualties were as follows:-

Sergeant Dahm, British South Africa Company was shot through the head, three of Khama's men were killed, and six or seven wounded. Sergeant-Major Codrington and Corporal Ransome, Bechuanaland Border Police, were slightly wounded, and Sergeant-Major Robertson and Sergeant Dempsey, British South Africa Company, also wounded, but not seriously. Two Bechuanaland Border Police horses and two British South Africa Company horses were shot.

On November 5th, Khama's natives, who had proved most useful to the expedition, left the column and voluntarily forfeited all claim to the pay of 1s. a day which they were to have received, as the terms of their contract with the British had not been fulfilled. Small-pox had broken out among their people and the King said that unless he could get back to his own country his folk would be dying in the veldt. It is highly probable that his little glimpse of active service had proved less to his liking than he had anticipated. Col. Goold-Adams entreated with him to lend his oxen and wagons, or at least to stay for a while, so that the Matabele would not witness his departure. But the chief was obdurate and departed at once with all his belongings, leaving the British with almost insufficient transport for the stores they carried.

But the difficulties were almost at an end. Within a few hours, the Colonel heard of the great victories of the Mashonaland columns, Lobengula's flight, and the general dispersal of the best of the impis; and on the 15th November, without further incident, the column arrived safely in Bulawayo, forming a junction with the forces under Major Forbes.

CHAPTER NINE

Official Appreciation of the B.B.P.
– Captain Coventry's report on the Shangani Patrol
– The Last of Major Allan Wilson

While the Tuli column had met with no very serious engagements, the march of Col. Goold-Adams and his men had been conducted in a most brilliant manner, and at the same time had given real service to the Mashonaland columns, for it had necessitated the drawing away from Mashonaland of 8,000 of Lobengula's fighting men; a force that might well have hindered Dr. Jameson and turned his expedition into a ghastly failure. The excellent work performed by the B.B.P. was recognised in the proper quarters and, in the course of a letter of appreciation to Col. Goold-Adams, the High Commissioner wrote the following:-

> I fully appreciate the difficulties which you had to encounter owing to the prolonged drought which had dried up the usual watering places and had burnt up the grass so that it was practically without nutriment for your horses and transport animals.
>
> The positions in your front were exceptionally strong, and as, owing to the drought, it was impossible to turn them you had to contemplate the probability of having to force them by a front attack.
>
> You had also to exercise caution, as in the case of a check or reverse to the British South Africa Company's Forces, you would have had to await Major Grey's reinforcements before proceeding to the relief of Dr. Jameson, and it was all important that you should not compromise or risk the safety of your force before your junction with Major Grey. I consider therefore, that you have carried out the military duty entrusted to you with zeal, ability and discretion and I have much pleasure in approving of your action.

The King had fled in the direction of the Bubi River and lay hiding somewhere in the neighbourhood. Dr. Jameson summoned him to surrender within two days and so save further bloodshed. At first Lobengula gave no reply, but subsequently he asked that two white traders whom he knew, Fairbairn and Asher, might be sent to treat with him, while he sent further to Dr. Jameson a second letter together with a present of gold dust. This letter fell into the hands of two criminal troopers of the Company's forces – Daniels and Wilson – who prevented it reaching its destination, in order that they might retain the gold for their own use. This act of treachery, surely the one dark blot on the hitherto unsullied annals of the country, proved afterwards to be a direct cause of the massacre of Allan Wilson and his noble little band. The crime was soon traced to the offenders, who were each sentenced to imprisonment for fourteen years.

Owing to the non arrival of the letter from Lobengula, the conclusion was made by Dr. Jameson that the King still held out, and in consequence a patrol of 300 men was formed, under Major Forbes, to pursue him. The B.B.P. were represented by a force of 90 officers and men, with four machine guns and three days' provisions, under the command of Captain Coventry. About this time it was thought advisable to bring into Matabeleland as many seasoned and disciplined troops as were available, and by December 15th the numbers of B.B.P. in the country were as follows:-

Captain Coventry and 80 officers and men with Major Forbes. Major Brown and 43 officers and men on detachment in the Matopos, with orders to accept all overtures to surrender on the part of the Matabele. (This force met with scarcely any opposition, the natives having, in almost all cases, agreed to make terms and return to their kraals.) At Bulawayo, 115 officers and men. Major Grey, with 125 officers and men, on detachment at Kumalo River. Lieut. Monro at Mangwe, with 28 men. En route to Mangwe, the balance of Major Grey's column, 120 officers and men. At Tati, 14 N.C.O.s and men.

Major Forbes' column left Bulawayo on the 14th November. The privations and difficulties endured by the men of the B.B.P. are described most vividly in the report written by Captain Coventry to his commanding officer, Col. Goold-Adams.

> 'We proceeded towards Inyati, and on the 16th, early in the morning, attacked the kopjes at the back of Inyati Mission Station, in the belief that there was an impi

there. This, however, was proved not to be the case. On the 17th, we left Inyati for the Bubi, and arrived there on the morning of the 18th. Messengers were sent from here to the King, and on the 19th a small party of Kaffirs came down and drove off some of the cattle that had been taken, frightening away our Makalaka boys. A party of 15 men, under Sub-Lieutenant Phipps, and the same number, under Capt. Francis, were sent after them. They captured the cattle and killed some of the natives. That same night two scouts Burnham and Ingram, were sent down the river with orders to fire off rockets; this they did and returned to camp. On the 20th Major Forbes decided to trek down the river some six or seven miles and then return. This was done. Whilst we were off-saddled four Matabele stalked one of our pickets and fired on it, they were shot. On the 21st we marched back to Inyati. I was in charge of a patrol of 45 men. We came across some Kaffirs in the thick bush who fired on us occasionally, we returning their fire, their loss being nine killed, none of my men were touched. That evening we arrived at Inyati. On the 23rd we left for Shiloh, and arrived there the same evening, meeting the column which had brought wagons and reinforcements, 200 dismounted men making our total strength about 500. On the 25th we marched from Shiloh, leaving behind us a good number of men, I cannot say the exact number, the seven-pounder gun, and some of the wagons, we proceeding with five wagons, and trekked on until the 28th. The roads were very heavy, and the progress of the wagons very slow. My horses began to get weak, I put this down to always being in the rear of the wagons and the badness of the grass, which was just sprouting and which did the horses no good and we could get no corn. On the 29th we left the wagons; they were to proceed to Inyati to await our return, they had with them sufficient garrison to occupy Inyati. I sent back 19 men and 11 horses which were unfit to proceed, our total strength being then about 160, I having 59 men and 73 horses and nine mules.

After our first trek to the Bembezi River I had to leave behind one horse, and after the second trek the same day I had to leave another, five more of my horses were knocked up. On the 30th more horses gave in and were left behind. In the afternoon we came across some Kaffirs, several of whom were taken with us. They appeared quite friendly, it was reported that there was a big stadt full of them near us. We reached the Bubi River the next day. Nothing of any importance occurred except the knocking up and leaving behind of horses, which happened every day until the 3rd December, when a shot was fired on our left flank. It was reported by the left flanking patrol. Later on that day we came to a piece of very open ground running down by the side of the Shangani with a big stadt to the right of the river, in which the King was supposed to have slept the previous night. I believe this to have been reported by a son of Magwegwi's, the induna of Bulawayo, who had been captured that afternoon. We crossed the King's wagon spoor and off-saddled near the river in the open space, having a good view all round us; previous to our off saddling Major Wilson had been ordered along the King's spoor in order to ascertain where it led to. At sundown he had not returned. Later in the night Captain Judd (Victoria Column) came into camp, his horse had been knocked up. He came from Major Wilson, I do not know what his report was.

This was the last sight the column had of the ill-fated Major and his party, whose story is too well known to the readers of this history.

CHAPTER TEN

Captain Coventry's Report Concluded
– Incessant Fighting – Privations of the Shangani
Patrol – Arrival at Inyati

'About midnight Captain Napier, Victoria Column, came into camp with a report from Major Wilson. What he reported I also do not know, but shortly afterwards Captain Borrow and some 15 or 20 men went out to reinforce Major Wilson. I heard afterwards that the message sent by Major Forbes to Major Wilson was to the effect that he (Major Wilson) must know his own position better than himself, and that he must use his own discretion. Captain Judd returned to Major Wilson with their party, Captain Napier stayed in camp. About this time we seemed to know, how I cannot say, that we were almost surrounded by the Matabele. On the morning of the 4th, as we were saddling up, shots were heard coming from the direction of Major Wilson's party. We marched down on the river, and after going about half a mile formed up for attack, the enemy opening fire on us from the bush on our left flank, about 400 yards off. We occupied some bushes in front of our horses, which gave the men sufficient cover, but was of no use to the horses. The firing continued for nearly an hour, when the enemy's fire was practically silenced. I should estimate the enemy at about 200, but as their line of fire was so extended and the bush thick, it is impossible to estimate accurately. Our casualties at this time were troopers Middleton and Shannahan slightly wounded, native driver, William Lefleur, badly wounded. Eight horses and one mule shot and wounded which afterwards had to be killed.

From here we commenced our retreat. It was not possible to advance, owing to the swollen state of the river, which had come down during the night, and which we should have had to cross in order to assist Major Wilson and his party. Also to transport our wounded men hampered us, and also the fact that the enemy were in force on the opposite bank of the river. Whilst we were retiring up the river to secure a good place to make a laager a few shots were fired at us by the enemy, wounding Lance-Corpl. Williams badly in the shoulder and Farrier-Corp. Newton very slightly indeed, one mule was also killed. We fortified ourselves in some bush on the bank of the river as strongly as possible. The enemy we could hear in the bush the other side of the river. Three or four tried to cross, but a shot or two stopped them. A rocket signal had been fired as a signal to Major Wilson. Four men that had gone with Major Wilson, and had been sent by him for reinforcements came in and informed Major Forbes of the condition of the party. That night rockets were sent up, and two men, Ingram and Lynch, were sent with despatches to Inyati. We marched the next morning, at about nine o'clock, up the river, the country being open. On the 6th two horses had knocked up, and I was obliged to shoot them and destroy the saddlery. On the 8th, when we were off-saddled, we were attacked by a small body of Matabele, who had come down after their cattle, which we had captured that morning. We fired at them and saddled up as soon as possible. Commandant Raff went into the bush to dislodge them, but they had beat their retreat before he had time to get to them. They succeeded in driving off their cattle. On the 10th we were again attacked by the Matabele. We had off-saddled under some kopjes, with a steep spruit on our left. One Maxim gun had been taken across the spruit, and the other was on the kopje side. The enemy had crept through our vedettes, and the first we knew of them was from the horse guard, several of the horses being stabbed by the enemy. The horses were driven into the spruit and we opened fire from the kopjes. Ten of the enemy were killed within 20 yards of the bigger of the two kopjes that we were holding on the left bank of the spruit. We also had some kopjes and ridges of rock on the right bank. Indunas were shouting out to their men to get round us, and to drop their guns and rush us with the assegai. This was not, however acted on. Though the enemy were at times quite close to us, we were unable to see them, owing to the denseness of the bush. We silenced their fire, however, and continued our march up the river, our casualties being Sgt. Gibson killed, and one horse, Bechuanaland Border Police. I do not know how many of the Company's horses were killed, but I saw about five or six.

As we were marching along, and after we had got a mile or so from the kopjes, we were again attacked. The firing commenced on our right flank. We formed up, owing to the thickness of the bush and the broken country the Maxims did not come into action at all. The firing was kept up entirely on our right flank and with rain falling heavily we silenced the enemy's fire. It was thought advisable to laager up where we were, so for the rest of the day we made as strong a scherm as we could. It was impossible to estimate the number of the enemy in either of these engagements. A council was held, when it was decided to leave the laager by night and march out of the kopjes and broken ground if possible, and to put as long a distance as possible between us and the enemy. We left the laager at 11 p.m. We had orders to leave behind any horses that were not really fit to go. This order I carried out, leaving 14 B.B.P. horses and two mules. These mules were perfectly fit, but I had a distinct order to leave them behind. The reasons given firstly, that one of them was always braying and that it would give the enemy notice of our retreat and secondly, that there were not enough men to leave them. The Maxim gun carriages were left behind here. On the morning of the 11th we came to some good open country, and formed laager shortly after sunrise. The distance covered along the river was not great, about 10 miles, but this was owing to the nature of the country. We had a second march that day of the same distance, and then off-saddled. All the men's rations had run out by this time. Three-quarter rations for 10 days having been taken from the wagons, some men had come to an end of theirs the day before and had had nothing to eat for 36 hours. We killed a horse here for the men to eat, and that night some of the men declared they saw a rocket. We signalled in return, but saw no answering signal. On the 12th we marched at dawn for about 8 miles and halted; from here four boys we sent up the river to the Hartley Hill Road to see if the wagons were there according to the message sent by Major Forbes through the two scouts Ingram and Lynch, to Inyati. If the wagons should prove not to be there, two boys were to push on along the road to Inyati and the other two boys were to come back and tell us. One boy, however, came back about an hour after they had started. Up to now we were deficient of 47 horses in the B.B. Police. We marched again that afternoon, and were again attacked. The enemy came down to the edge of the bush. We were five or six hundred yards from the bank of the river at this time. The Maxims immediately opened fire, and the horses were taken down to the river to be under cover. The Maxims retired to the bank of the river, we keeping up our fire on the enemy, when we in turn retired. Sgt. Pyke, B.B.P. was wounded in the right arm whilst serving one Maxim, and Tpr. Nesbit, B.S.A.Co. was wounded in the forearm. We then retired up the river and got into a very good position, the enemy following us up, and every now and again exchanging shots across a bend in the river some 800 yards away, but the Maxim silenced them. A small party, evidently of the enemy, crossed the river and fired at us from the opposite bank, but were soon silenced by the Maxim. We could not estimate the number of the enemy here or their loss, but a good number of them were killed. That night we marched again, and on the 13th crossed the river for the first time. This was done in order to pass some very dangerous ground – kopjes chiefly – that were just on the bank of river, and which I am absolutely certain the Matabele were in, as I saw several of them on the rocks. We crossed the river again and formed laager. That night at dark we marched again, and crossed a spruit which some of the boys declared to be the Longwe, so we ringed our horses and waited until daylight, and when it came we looked for a suitable place to form camp whilst waiting for our messengers to return from the road. As we were looking for a suitable place Commandant Raaf saw the Longwe River ahead of us, so we crossed the river and encamped. Before this we had passed a Maholi kraal of three huts. These Maholi came across the river to us and gave us two cows, which were at once killed for rations. He also promised to lead us up the Longwe to the road, so saving a good deal of the distance. The two boy messengers here returned and reported that the wagons were not at the drift, so we marched for Inyati that afternoon, the Maholi acting as guide. We off saddled at 5.30, and Mr. Selous and Mr. Accutt joined us, telling us that they had left the wagons which had been sent from Inyati to our relief only a mile and a half away. They had trekked across the veldt for the junction of the Longwe, the third messenger having made his way into Inyati and having given information as to our whereabouts. We marched on to the wagons, and on the 15th arrived at Inyati, having marched 22 miles that day with the wagons.

Our total loss of horses, B.B. Police, was as follows: killed in action, 9; killed by order, 7; left behind, 36, of which 14 were left in laager; shot for food, 1; total 53 and 4 mules. Two of these horses have since been recovered. The men stood the hardships of the march wonderfully. There was no grumbling, and every man did his duty. The majority of them had not boots that were fit for service, and some had to make sandals or slippers out of wallets. Their feet were in an awful state. It rained every day bar one since leaving Inyati, the men had no great coats, and some of them had to leave their blankets behind. The wounded men, Lance-Corpl. Williams and native driver Lefleur, were carried on the Maxim carriages until we left these behind. They then had to ride, as also did Sgt. Pyke. It must have been terrible for these three poor fellows. The other men were only slightly wounded, and riding was easy for them. I regret to have to announce the death of native driver William Lefleur, which occurred on the 2nd from the effects of his wound.'

CHAPTER ELEVEN

The War Ended – Formation of the Matabeleland Mounted Police – Clive would have Done It – Preparing for the Jameson Raid

The meeting of Major Forbe's patrol with Dr. Jameson and his relieving force made the opportunity for the first restful night's sleep the men of the B.B.P. had enjoyed for some months, with no fear of disturbance by hostile Matabele. On the following morning, the united force trekked, in the heaviest of rains, for Bulawayo, which they gained in three days. Shortly afterwards, they received the welcome news that Lobengula had died of dysentery in his wagon on the banks of the Shangani. The King's death broke the power of the Matabele, hostilities came to an end almost at once, and the leading indunas hastened to Bulawayo to sue for peace. To the B.B.P. fell one of the most honourable duties the Police have ever been called upon to perform, the finding and burial of the bodies of the heroes that had fallen by the side of Major Allan Wilson.

On December 23rd 1893, the entire British force that had been engaged in the war paraded in Bulawayo before Mr. Rhodes, who lauded them in most glowing words for the work they had done, and the courage and cheerfulness they had shown in overcoming the tremendous difficulties that had confronted them. The Volunteer regiments were disbanded, and the B.B.P. set out from Bulawayo on their return to the South. Their work during the campaign had been carried through without a flaw; they had been the only properly disciplined troops to take the field; and it was through them especially that the founding of the white man's rule in Matabeleland had been made possible.

On the conclusion of the war, a new regular force, the Matabeleland Mounted Police, was formed to protect the settlers from stray bands of hostile Matabele that still lurked in the Matopos and along the lower Shangani. This corps, 150 strong, was associated with the old Mashonaland Police as a branch of the B.S.A. Co.'s Police. Command was given to Lieutenant Bodle. At the same time an armed force of Native

Police was raised for the purpose of getting into better touch with the native inhabitants of the country, and ensuring that the orders of the Native Commissioners were carried out. For a while peace reigned throughout the Company's territories, a period of steady development lasting nearly two years commenced, and nothing happened to advertise the labours of the Rhodesian Police until the world famous fiasco of the Jameson Raid came about to put back the growth of the new country, and, incidentally, to set ablaze both Matabeleland and Mashonaland with all the horrors of a more or less concerted native rising.

The prologue of the drama which we know as the Jameson Raid has been described most vividly by an eyewitness. The story is absolutely authentic:

> The scene is the stoep of Government House, Bulawayo. The leading actor is His Honour Leander Starr Jameson, M.D., C.B., Administrator of Matabeleland. The time is one of great unrest, with tales of oppression and injustice pouring all over the Empire from the mouths and pens of the large body of Britishers who labour in the gold mines around Johannesburg. The Imperialist papers, British and South African, are crying aloud their complaints and remedies, and but a slight touch of the torch is wanting to set the pile of discontent alight. The doctor has in his hands a cigarette which he is smoking, and a *Life of Clive* which he reads attentively. Suddenly he looks up from the book and exclaims: 'I have a jolly good mind to march straight down the plateau with the men I have here, and settle the thing out of hand. The idea of South Africa going on being trodden upon by this Pretoria gang is absurd. I have a good mind to get the fellows together and start to-morrow, via Tati.'
>
> A companion suggests that there are, at the most, a couple of hundred Matabeleland Mounted Police available, that it would take them at least three weeks to carry out the proposed programme, and that meanwhile the international situation would be somewhat peculiar, probably resulting in the disbandment of the regiment by cable.
>
> 'You may say what you like,' says the man of action, 'but Clive would have done it.' That seems to be the origin of the whole muddle and mystery of the Raid: 'Clive would

have done it.'

The original plan of the would be revolutionists was as follows: The British party in Johannesburg was to form an ultimatum and follow it up by force sufficient to take the town and declare itself a Provisional Government. The same night a surprise visit to Pretoria was to be made, and the final coup accomplished without firing a shot. Downing Street had already been sounded as to its probable actions, but the malcontents had been assured that Great Britain could not interfere in the internal affairs of the Transvaal on their behalf, and could only act afterwards by way of keeping the peace in South Africa, and not at a time or in a way which could be construed as assisting to break it. Hence the border was looked to. It was thought that Rhodesia could do best for Great Britain what Great Britain was unable to do for herself. Rhodesia's sympathies were entirely with the Uitlanders, she had already (in Manicaland) shown her disregard for official red tape, and at the worst she could create a diversion providing the breathing space that might force the hand of the Home authorities.

The weak points of this fine scheme are obvious now, but at that time nobody doubted that Rhodesia was to prove in some way the hope of the Britishers in South Africa. And, as a matter of fact, had the Uitlanders in the Transvaal only worked together and shown the energy and enterprise that was displayed by the Rhodesian police, ruling power in Pretoria must inevitably have fallen to their hands. But racial feeling among themselves, aided by the nervous haste of Dr. Jameson, was to prove the principal cause of the great failure. The 'Flag question' lay at the root of the whole trouble.

What was to be the ultimate future of the Transvaal? The country should lie under the Flag of England said the Britishers, but the Africander revolutionists disagreed: while the large body of Americans, inflamed at the time by the Venezuelan affair and President Cleveland's bellicose threats, refused to have anything to do with an emblem so officially British as the Union Jack, and stood out for the old Republican 'vier kleur.' The consequence of all this was that when the Rhodesians did move, the Uitlander's plans fizzled out like a damp squib, and no help at all was forthcoming for Dr. Jameson and his little band.

At the time when the energetic Doctor decided to act on his own responsibility and put into practice his characteristic rule of 'shoving things through,' he had behind him a military force of under 600, all told. These lay at Pitsani, Pothlugo and Mafeking, the three places being about 27 miles apart. The camp at Pitsani had been formed ostensibly for the purpose of 'protecting' the railway works. From the 20th to the 31st October 1895, the M.M.P. were being drafted there from Bulawayo, in all 250 men, 293 horses, 168 mules, six Maxims, and two field guns. On the 15th November the Imperial authorities, in handing over a portion of Bechuanaland Protectorate to the Company, proceeded to disband the B.B.P., a force of much sterner material than that of the Old Company's Police, numbering a few hundred. The majority of these were re-enlisted by the M.M.P. These troops were added to further by a small number of picked men from the Colonial Volunteers (Duke of Edinburgh's Own), who hastened up from Cape Town at the instigation of Dr. Jameson. At Mafeking, there were stationed about 160 or 170 men, including two troops which were still officially Bechuanaland Border Police.

Besides Dr. Jameson, the principal officers taking part in the Raid were as follows: Lieut. Col. Sir John Willoughby (Major, Royal Horse Guards), in general military command; Major the Hon. Robert White (Captain, Royal Welsh Fusiliers); Lieut. Col. the Hon. Henry F. White (Major, Grenadier Guards), in charge of M.M.P.; Lieut. Col. Raleigh Grey (Captain, 6th Dragoons), in charge of B.B.P.; the Hon. C.J. Coventry (a Militia officer), and several officers of the Guards. The officers, for the most part, formed a jovial, careless troop of titled young ne'er-do-wells, such as might have found their place in the ranks of Prince Rupert's fighting horse, and they have often been justly contrasted with the dour, religious old 'Ironsides' who were to give them their Dunbar. Sir John Willoughby was the most experienced of the lot. He had already served as military adviser to Jameson during the Matabele War and had endeared himself to his followers as the holder of one of the finest hunting reputations in England and a Derby winner.

Of the troopers, about one half were, more or less, seasoned irregulars. There were the ex-B.B.P. who formed the backbone of the column. The M.M.P. were almost all youngsters of 18 or 20. Many had just arrived from home and have been quite green but for the little drilling they had received in camp during the last few weeks. They had not had time to learn to ride, for the Boers, after the surrender, were astonished to find the breeches of many of them sticking to the saddle with blood! The column held a sprinkling of Africanders, some of them with the typical Franco-Dutch names.

The force of 600 included seventy odd native transport boys. One hundred thousand rounds of rifle ammunition were carried, besides 45,000 rounds for the Maxims, and about 120 for each of the other guns.

CHAPTER TWELVE

The Start of the Raid – How they cut the Wire
– The Order of March – A Challenge
– The High Commissioner's Despatch

On the afternoon of Sunday, December 29th, the troops at Mafeking and Pitsani were paraded before their respective leaders. At Pitsani the men were addressed by Dr. Jameson, Col. White and Sir John Willoughby, while at Mafeking the speakers were Col. Grey and Major Coventry. Many of the troopers now heard of their true destination for the first time. They had been told that their previous hard drilling had been given them in preparation for a police raid on an insubordinate petty chief in the neighbourhood, but as Major Coventry told them: 'We cannot keep it from you any longer. It is all bosh about fighting Linchwe. We are going straight to Johannesburg. We want you all to come. It will be a short trip, everything has been arranged for'. A few of the listeners were inclined to hang back on learning the truth, and some of them asked whether they were to march under orders of the Queen or the Company. 'I cannot say that you are going under the Queen's orders,' said Col. Grey, frankly, 'but I do say that you are going to fight for the supremacy of the British Flag in South Africa.'

At Pitsani, the men had been prepared for news of this nature by the gossip relating to the affairs of the Transvaal, which had prevailed in the district. Dr. Jameson appealed to their spirit of chivalry by reading a letter signed by five Johannesburgers and asking for help for the women and children who were in danger: Further, he assured them that they need have no fear of being left to fight their way alone. There were two thousand armed Britishers in Johannesburg; C.M.R. and the Rhodesian Horse would not be slow in coming to the rescue, while on the news of the engagement reaching the South, help could be relied upon from the Imperial forces in Natal. A bonus would be given to those who had taken an active part in the Raid, and now was the time for those who were weak-hearted to fallout and stay at Pitsani. The answer to this appeal was a spontaneous burst of cheering from the delighted youngsters, eager all of them to ride on an adventure that seemed to be born of Old World romance, originated by their proper authorities, and led by such an able and experienced adventurer as Dr. Jim. The start of the raiding column has been described by Inspector Fuller, of the Cape Police, who was surprised at supper in Mafeking by volleys of cheering which came from the direction of the Police Barracks.

Hastening to the spot, he saw that the men were being paraded in full marching order, he noted Col. Grey rallying some troopers who seemed reluctant to fall in, and proceeded to investigate. He reports:-

> I followed the column on foot and found that they were taking the main road to the Protectorate, but seeing a cart and six mules belonging to the Company move off in the direction of the Buurman's Drift Road to the Transvaal, I took a short cut on to this road. When I got about half way between these two roads, I heard the command given to form to the right, and then someone, I was too far off to recognise the voice, or distinguish the words, made what I thought was a short speech, after which a cheer was given, and column of route was again formed. The head of the column then wheeled to the right, left the Protectorate road just past the township, and came into the Transvaal road where I was standing. I estimated the numbers as they passed me in the moonlight to be about 160 men, with four guns. As Major White passed me he bade me good-bye. I returned the greeting, and told him at the same time that I was reporting the whole affair. He said. 'It's all right old chap, you can do what you like, the wires are cut.'

But here the gallant Major was wrong. It was true that one wire, the southward one to the Colony was cut south of Pitsani and again south of Mafeking, but the really important wire, running to Pretoria by way of Zeerust and Rustenburg, was left untouched. And thereby hangs one of the many ludicrous tales which form such undignified appendices to the story of the Raid. A trooper was dispatched with most minutely detailed instructions to cut the wire in two places, so many yards apart, take it so far into the veldt, and bury it so deep. Unfortunately, the warrior conceived the idea that the acquisition of a little Dutch courage would be necessary if he was to carry out his orders in a proper manner and, to put it plainly, he became very drunk while proceeding to the scene of operations. Eventually, he did cut a wire, and he did bury it in the veldt, but the wire that had attracted his attention happened to be part of a railing which had been used for the enclosure of a herd of cattle.

The route taken by the column lay along a plain wagon road nearly the whole way to Krugersdorp. Four stores were passed and a few homesteads. There was also a canteen of some sort for every two hours of the march, and, out of this fact, cynical Boers have woven countless legends relating to the expedition which, though highly ingenious, are wholly imaginary. The distance from Mafeking to Krugersdorp is about 130 miles. The order of march had been detailed as carefully as the route, which had been studied months before by the indefatigable Major 'Bobby' White. Scouts, advance guard and flanking columns had been thrown out, while the artillery and scotch carts moved in the centre. The following is a copy of instructions signed by J. Willoughby, Colonel, O.C. Column:-

ORDERS FOR INTELLIGENCE IN CHARGE OF SCOUTS (SPECIAL PARTY)

1. A party of 12 picked men will be detailed for advanced patrol.
2. Captain Lindsell will be in charge, six men will be employed and accompany him unless more are detailed.
3. Captain Lindsell's party will always start half an hour by day and a quarter of an hour by night before the column moves off.
4. He will report himself to O.C. Column before moving off.
5. This party marches independent of the main body, and will regulate its pace to about five miles per hour.
6. The party will halt at places named by O.C. Column.
7. One man of the party will march about 100 yards ahead of the remainder and one man 100 yards in rear.
8. A guide will accompany the party.
9. The officer in charge will endeavour to obtain all the information he can of the road ahead, and will warn all stores of the approach of the column, so that forage and food may be prepared ready for issue on the arrival of the column. He will inform persons he may meet that if they keep quiet they will not be molested in any way, and that the column has no hostile intentions against

the inhabitants of the country. In case of any hostile demonstration he is to fall back, sending back a message with the fullest information as to the nature of such, and any important information as to any movement of armed bodies should also be sent to the O.C. Column, stating whether the information be hearsay or otherwise, and from whom obtained.

The message should state exact time, place of its despatch, if possible in writing.

This party is not to scout to the flanks, as this will be done by the advanced guard, but caution must be exercised in approaching a village, defile, or any awkward piece of country.

Ascertain about water, how far, and how many horses can be watered at the same time. See that water is boiled for coffee, etc.

The march was carried out as speedily as possible, the column walking, cantering and trotting by turns. There were no rests to enable the men to sleep, 'off-saddles' being just long enough to ease the horses and let the riders sit down for a while before going off again. For some reason no halts were made at the four stores, so that the troops were unable to obtain the 'bully' and biscuits which had been previously procured for them. Two hours was the longest halt of any kind, except once, when the road was lost in the dark.

The first challenge came on Monday from the Commandant of the Marico district to the 'Head officer of the expedition of armed troops at Malmani Eye,' warning him to re-cross the frontier and not to act against the law of the land, the Convention, and international law. In reply, Jameson wrote: 'I intend proceeding with my original plans, which have no hostile intentions against the people of the Transvaal, but we are here in reply to an invitation from the principal residents of the Rand and to assist them in their demands for justice and the ordinary rights of every citizen of a civilized State.'

On Tuesday morning the raiders reached the farm of Mr. Malan, a member of the Volkraad and close relation of General Joubert. He expressed his anger and surprise in strong terms to Jameson, but of course had no power to stay the column. A little later a mounted messenger arrived from Mafeking, after a hard ride of 80 miles, during which he had been captured by a party of Boers on the border, who had assembled for the purpose of stopping any supports that might be following the column. This trooper carried a despatch which had been forwarded by the High Commissioner to the Resident Commissioner at Mafeking. In a separate communication for each officer in the column there was a copy of this despatch. Jameson was ordered to return immediately, and warned that the violation of the territory of a friendly State was repudiated by Her Majesty's Government. The officers were told that they were rendering themselves liable to severe penalties. But the leaders of the column, guessing the nature of these orders, were in no hurry to read them. The first officer addressed by the messenger bade him to carry the despatches to Sir John Willoughby. Willoughby referred the trooper to Jameson. The Doctor ordered him to take them back to Sir John Willoughby, he is in military command. In the end the messenger was told that the despatches would be attended to, and the column went forward once more.

CHAPTER THIRTEEN

The Absent Convoy – The Spider and the Fly
– Doornkop – Jameson Hoists the White Flag
– The Prisoners in Pretoria

The old commando system of mobilisation was yet again to prove an ideal one when practised by the ready and warlike citizen of the Transvaal. It was not possible for Jameson to continue his march much longer without a check. At Krugersdorp, some fifteen miles from Johannesburg he was confronted by a Boer force of 1,500 men, the first body of Burghers to assemble on the news that the raiding column had crossed the frontier. On the Tuesday night a small party of Boers had fired on the column, slightly wounding a couple of troopers, but it was here the real fighting commenced, at one a.m. on New Year's Day, and here the impetuous Doctor came to realise, more bitterly than ever, the extent of the blunders and mismanagement committed by himself and everyone else connected with the starting of the raid. It had been arranged that four wagon loads of supplies, together with 250 horses and 100 mules, should be sent out from Johannesburg to meet the Raiders at Krugersdorp, but as it happened the whole lot fell into the hands of the Boers at Reit Spruit, some distance away, after the fighting was finished. Two thousand Uitlanders, armed and mounted, were to have acted as a convoy for the wagons, but at Krugersdorp they also were conspicuous by their absence. There was only one message of any sort received from the sympathisers in the city, and that took the form of a note from the Defence Committee, saying an armistice with the President had been concluded until the High Commissioner had been up to Pretoria, and that therefore Jameson and his followers could expect no assistance from Johannesburg. With a gesture of absolute disgust, the Doctor tore the paper to pieces, declaring that he for one had done with Johannesburg.

Probably by this time the leading Britishers knew that their task was a hopeless one. The idea of the gallant little column cutting its way into the heart of the Rand without the slightest chance of securing outside help had never been considered but a very large part of the invaders had been recruited from the Public Schools of England, while all were keen sportsmen. Britishers and Colonials alike, to them it seemed that the risks they had to meet made the whole game really worth playing. Famished and weary as they were, they went in to play the game, and win it if they could. But every man was quite prepared to die.

As soon as Jameson had approached sufficiently near to communicate with the residents of Krugersdorp, he gave notice that he intended to take the town, and warned the women and children to leave. His haste was somewhat premature, for it was fated that none of his followers were to enter the town at all except as captives.

The main road ran between two large kopjes. These were both held by strong bodies of Boers, who had decided to employ the tactics which had always proved of such service to them in their Native Wars, it was the old game of the spider and the fly. Little groups would advance towards the ground held by the column, only to retreat again and so lead the pursuing Raiders towards the neighbourhood of the place where they had taken up their main positions. There they had the unwary Britishers at their mercy. They could do no damage, beyond throwing a few shells into the town or the court-house, while the Boers were able to greet them with a fusillade which speedily rendered their position untenable. The fighting raged in the midst of a terrific thunderstorm. Followed by a hot fire, Jameson turned to try another road which passed through Randfontein. There two troopers were killed, but still the Boers waited, reserving the final attack till the arrival of fresh commandoes. Beyond Brink's farmhouse at Doornkop, they were posted in large numbers on both sides of the road, and by sunset Jameson was completely surrounded. During the night the commandoes had swollen to an army of 4,000 men, all mounted and armed with the Martini-Henry. Their ammunition had been reinforced by means of special trains from Johannesburg. The Defence Committee did make some show of action by blowing up the line between Langlaate and Krugersdorp, but their sudden enthusiasm was too late, the supplies already having been sent. The only result of the move was that the feeling of warlike animosity on the part of the Boers was brought to the pitch of personal hatred, while Jameson himself in no way benefited. The column stood at bay on a small kopje which occupied the centre of a cup-like valley. From four sides the enemy overlooked them from the summits of larger hills. The Britishers were disposed in the form of a rough hexagonal laager, the horses and wagons occupying the inside, while the men lay outside, shoulder to shoulder.

There was a Maxim at each corner. Twice the column was attacked during the actual process of making the laager, but the Boers, as usual, did not shine at direct attack and there was no loss incurred on either side. Once again, at nine o'clock, the burghers attempted to rush the position but without result. Through the night the Britishers attempted to shell the Boer position, trying to find the hidden marksmen by the use of an electric searchlight, but the effort was in vain. Concealed by huge boulders and protected by the rising ground the Boers lay in perfect security. The British guns were constantly jamming, particularly the Maxims, while men and horses were dropping from sheer exhaustion. The troopers had been in the saddle almost continuously during the four days trek; once they had ridden 150 miles in less than 40 hours. Many of them had fallen asleep during the brief rests, with their rifles in one hand and the reins in the other.

Just before dawn it was obvious to their leaders that they had fallen into a trap, and that the only thing to do was to make the attempt to dash through the lines of Boer marksmen. The command was given to break up the laager. While the order was being carried out, the Boers charged for the fourth time, with the result that three men of the column were killed and several wounded. At five o'clock the column was well away at a fast canter, and for three hours a brisk running fight was kept up. But large bodies of Boers kept the hills, where they could not be over-looked, and at eight o'clock Major Coventry was sent out to meet them hand to hand. His men charged with all the gallantry and spirit that they had shown since leaving Mafeking, and did succeed in capturing the kopje which they had made their chief objective. But behind this lay another, strongly entrenched, while more Boers peopled the kopjes on all sides of the attacking force. Meanwhile the ammunition was running short. One of the two wagon loads had fallen too far in the rear of the column and fell into the hands of the enemy. The guns were almost useless and about this time a message was received from Sir Jacobus de Wet, the British Resident, ordering Dr. Jameson's followers to retire beyond the border.

The unhappy Doctor probably wished at this time he could give literal effect to the order, but at any rate he saw that further resistance was not only useless, but would involve terrible futile bloodshed, and at 9 o'clock he hoisted the white flag.

For some little time the Boers refused to take notice of this signal, and indeed fired at least one deliberate volley. The men of the column wished to fight on to the end and many of them were openly crying and cursing, when ordered by their officers to lay down their arms. However, the Doctor was firm, and the men were drawn up in troops in the form of a square, piling their rifles in the centre. Then the Boers came down in a rush, capturing the whole force, with the rifles and what ammunition remained. From first to last the fighting had gone on for 36 hours over an area of 25 miles. It is difficult to estimate the actual losses. The Transvaal Government instituted a censorship of all press and private telegrams, most of which were mutilated prior to transmission. The first cabled reports stated that no less than 240 of Jameson's men had been killed outright, but later it was announced officially that 130 had been killed and 39 wounded, while the Boers had only lost three killed and six wounded. The Raiders themselves, on their return to England in February, admitted the loss of 20 men, but asserted that they must have killed and wounded at least 270 Boers. The one fact certain that the stolid farmers who composed the Burgher force had lost their boasted skill in shooting since the thinning out of the buck in their country, for taking all their advantages of position and readiness into consideration, the British losses should have been tremendous.

The wounded men were placed in Brink's farmhouse, which was converted into a hospital. There they were tended, Boers and Britishers together by sisters of mercy, who had come from Krugersdorp for the purpose. Many civilians from the town had watched the whole fight with eager anxiety, and these people assisted in burying the dead, with large parties of Kaffirs from the mines. The other prisoners were marched into Krugersdorp. Some of them were so exhausted that they were unable to sit on their horses. They were all well-nigh fainting for want of food, and they had not tasted anything for over twenty-four hours. Their conquerors behaved in a most humane manner, procuring all the food available for the prisoners and, in every way, showing the greatest consideration for their weariness and natural dejection.

A soon as possible the column was escorted to Pretoria by an enormous host of jubilant Boers. They arrived in the capital on the Friday night and took up their quarters on the English racecourse. At first the feeling of animosity displayed by the citizens ran to fever heat. It is certain that, had it not been for the firmness and tact of the Dutch commandant, both Jameson and Willoughby would have been shot in the public square. Most of the troopers fully expected that was to be the fate of them all, but, as it fell out, only two of them who were proved to be citizens of the Transvaal, both having served as gunners in the Staats Artillerie, were shot. The rest were treated kindly. Each man was provided with a Kaffir blanket and, before finally quitting the Transvaal, with a suit of clothes, shirt and boots. After a short time, the people began to recognise that their hatred should be reserved for the craven folk in Johannesburg, who had misled the Rhodesians. The police they respected as brave men who had done what they thought to be their duty, and they showed their appreciation by bringing the captives little presents of tobacco, for which the men were highly grateful.

CHAPTER FOURTEEN

Dr. Jameson and his Officers Sentenced to Imprisonment – World-Wide Excitement – The Kaiser puts his Foot into it – Captain Thatcher – Johannesburg to Blame – The South African Committee and its Conclusions

Jacobus de Wet, the British Agent in Pretoria, proved quite unequal to the situation that confronted him on the surrender of the Raiders. In an endeavour to calm the leaders of the Reform Party in Johannesburg, he stated that he could guarantee that neither the Raiders nor the Reformers should have a hair of their heads touched, and promised that the Transvaal Government would grant the needed reforms. As a matter of fact the President wished for some time to make an end of Dr. Jameson and everyone of his Officers and only consented to hand them over to the British authorities on the receipt of a dignified message from the Colonial Secretary, Mr. Joseph Chamberlain, appealing to his clemency. Probably there would even now have arisen a tremendous upheaval on the Rand had it not been for the tactful conduct of the High Commissioner, who warned Kruger against the consequences of a threatened attack of Johannesburg, and hurried up himself from Cape Town to prove to the President the real good faith of the Home Government.

On the arrival of the officers of the raiding party in England, Dr. Jameson was smuggled up the Thames in the police steamer, and landed at Waterloo Bridge, hereby avoiding the demonstration that would have ensued on his recognition by the populace. But he and his comrades received a most enthusiastic greeting in Bow Street, and at the Court next day, when they were charged under the Foreign Enlistment Act. On July 20th, they were brought to the bar for trial before Lord Chief Justice Russell, Baron Pollock, and Mr. Justice Hawkins. There they were found guilty, as Lord Russell had directed in a strong and comprehensive speech, but the jury accompanied their finding with a rider that the state of things in Johannesburg presented great provocation. Dr. Jameson was sentenced to fifteen months imprisonment, Sir John Willoughby to ten, Major Robert White to seven, Colonel Henry White and Major Coventry to five, all without hard labour. The last however, who was suffering from the severe wound he had received at Doornkop, was released almost at once and the Doctor, whose health had been gravely endangered in prison, was released early in December. The men had previously been allowed to return to their homes by the President of the Transvaal.

For a long time, the interest and excitement consequent on the news of the battle of Krugersdorp stirred discussion and wrangling almost to fever heat, not only in England, but all over the civilized world. The Poet Laureate expressed the feeling of the greater part of Britishers in a poem to the *Times* which, while it was probably stirring enough to people whose whole public interest still lay in the Raid, can only be read now as an extraordinary sample of pseudo-patriotic doggerel. The German Emperor was, as usual, quick to 'put his foot into things' generally. Immediately he heard of the defeat of the Raiders, he wired to Kruger: 'I express to you my sincere congratulations that without appealing to the help of friendly Powers you and your people have succeeded in repelling with your own forces the armed bands which had broken into your country and in maintaining the independence of your country against foreign aggression.'

The Kaiser further besought permission from Portugal to land marines at Delagoa Bay 'for the protection of German interests' but this was curtly declined. The action was a most uncalled for piece of German bombast, recognizing, as it did, a country which was nominally under British suzerainty as an independent Power and even Kruger himself replied with no show of encouragement. England for her part, prepared for a European war. The South African forces were strengthened, the admiral on the Cape station sailed for Delagoa Bay, and a flying squadron assembled at Spithead in complete readiness to go to sea. The Kaiser, who was undoubtedly unprepared for this display of readiness, despatched his now famous letter of apology to the Queen, the German Press followed suit with columns of exaggerated explanation and goodwill, and the Foreign Minister expressly disavowed to the British Ambassador any hostility to Great Britain. As President Kruger afterwards put it, the menace disappeared 'when the old lady sneezed.' Meanwhile, England was overcome by the spontaneous outburst of loyalty from the Colonies, which rallied unanimously to the Mother Country in what a Canadian statesman termed her 'splendid isolation.'

Among the many rumours and tall stories that were rife in London, previous to the arrival of the prisoners from the Transvaal, there were some curious statements floated by one Thatcher who described himself as a Captain in the Police. They were received at first with much enthusiasm by the London Press, and the *Illustrated London News* published as a supplement a complete number telling the story of the Raid as chronicled by Capt. Thatcher. This man stated that he had been entrusted with the charge of one of the Column's Maxims, that he had acted as galloper for Jameson, and that had he been allowed to have his own way he could have secured the assistance of 500 Johannesburgers and held the Boers in check. He had been captured, he said, but had managed to get away with the aid of an Englishman who was engaged in the secret service of the Transvaal. But the history of the Jameson Raid was not to be made in this manner. In the *Times* of February 25th, 1896, there appeared a letter signed by W. Bodle, Chief Inspector of Police, and the following Inspectors of the M.M.P., Lawson, L.B. Dykes, Frank L. Bowden, M. Straker, and G.V. Drury. These officers stated that, on arrival at Las Palmas, en route for England,

> they were vastly surprised to find various accounts of Dr. Jameson's march, fights, etc., contributed to your columns, and to those of other papers, by an individual describing himself as Captain Thatcher.
>
> These statements published in a less influential organ than the *Times* would not be worth refuting, but as the case stands the public should not be misled further by the man's pretensions and utterly unreliable statements. He was recognised by one of our officers at Malmani on the line of march, as an ex-corporal of the 17th Lancers, who succeeded in obtaining a commission, but for some reason or other he left the service shortly after.
>
> Some fifty miles from our starting point he had galloped after and caught us up, apparently in a fright, stating that Boers were in rear of us, which was perfectly untrue. Here he was allowed to remain with the column, as he begged hard for that privilege, but was suspected as being a spy

and treated as such. He rode with the column until we reached Krugersdorp, after which he disappeared.

The letter went on to deny almost every one of the statements the gallant 'Captain' had made, and concluded with a request that the editor should give publicity to the facts with the object of exposing an imposter. And so this modern relation of the Ancient Pistol had to discard the hero's cloak which he had worn in the eyes of the credulous British public, and eat the leek of satire which they hastened to bring before him.

While dealing with the story of the Great Fiasco we have confined ourselves as far as possible to the part taken by the Police and their immediate commanders, and left untouched the other tale of the political plots and counter plots which led up to the crisis. But the rights and wrongs of the whole question may best be gleaned by a study of the conduct of the Johannesburgers after Dr. Jameson had shown his activity. There is no doubt at all that these fatuous conspirators, 100,000 of them, had led the Rhodesians to believe that their help was absolutely essential and that at once, and, there is no doubt that the Doctor and his followers had put complete faith in the stories, many of them exaggerated, or untrue, that had reached them, of suffering and persecution among the Uitlander population of the Rand. The whole justification of the conspiracy, if there was one, lay in ultimate success, yet when the little band of Police had been lured over the frontier to the rescue of the wives and children of the great crowd of foreigners that cried to them from Johannesburg, the plotters made not the slightest attempt to redeem their valiant promises, they never stirred an inch outside the town, and they allowed Jameson to battle for the lives of his men against an overwhelming army, within fifteen miles of Johannesburg, without making the slightest attempt to assist him in any way. With their cowardice, they had converted what might have been at least a decent revolution into a mere filibustering expedition. As one distinguished Imperialist, Sir Gilbert Parker, has said: 'The Johannesburg conspirators who had bungled their side of the business had certainly shown no rashness. At any rate, whatever the merits of the case, no one in England accused the Johannesburgers of foolhardy courage or impassioned daring. They were so busy in trying to induce Jameson to go back that they had no time to go forward themselves. It was not that they lost their heads, their hearts were the disappearing factors.'

The final and most logical conclusions on the subject of the Jameson Raid were arrived at by the South African Committee which met on February 16th. There Mr. Rhodes catalogued the grievances of the Uitlanders and the corruption of the Boers, and admitted that 'acting within my rights' he had placed a body of troops under Dr. Jameson, prepared to act in certain eventualities. The Doctor had, however, gone in without his authority. The latter gave a candid narrative of the events of the Raid, stated that his move had been precipitated by a Reuters telegram, dated December 28th, speaking of the secret arming and warlike preparations of Johannesburg, and added naively that he felt sure all would be forgiven him in the event of success. In the end it was decided by the Committee that great discontent had existed for some time in Johannesburg, and that Mr. Rhodes had acted without any justification in using the forces and resources of the Chartered Company to support a revolution, and his heavy responsibility remained. It was admitted that Jameson had actually 'gone in' without Mr. Rhodes' authority and, to use 'the Peacemaker's' own words, had 'upset his apple cart'. Two of the Company's directors were censured, as being aware of all that was going on, the Colonial Secretary had not been aware of the plot during its development and was not in any way to be held responsible, and finally the Committee wished to put on record an absolute condemnation of the Raid. Mr. Chamberlain, in the House of Commons, pronounced a personal and effusive eulogy upon Mr. Rhodes saying, amid the wildest enthusiasm from the Members, though his fault was as about as great as any politician could commit, he had done nothing that affected his character as a man of honour.

We cannot conclude this narrative without a reference to the incident which put the finishing touch to the long list of absurdities which had accompanied the story of the Raid. Kruger claimed on account of the invasion of his territory the colossal sum of £1,677,938.3s.3d. One item of a million sterling was for the moral and intellectual damage.

CHAPTER FIFTEEN

The Withdrawal of the M.M.P. and its Results – Other Causes of the Outbreak of '96 – A Desperate Situation – The First Murder at Umgorshlwini

The withdrawal from Matabeleland of the M.M.P. that participated in the Jameson Raid led directly to the most disastrous period of history that Rhodesia has yet known. Many causes have been assigned to the outbreak of '96, with, of course, the usual additions and embellishments from the highly imaginative 'Little England' Party at Home, but the one real reason lay in the absence of the only organised and disciplined fighting force possessed by the British in Rhodesia, and the consequent spirit of defiance and self confidence which was exhibited by the Matabele. Without a doubt the natives at the time had their grievances, real and imaginary. Since 1890, the first year of the occupation of Mashonaland, the whole of the country had been afflicted by a plague of locusts; for two years prior to the rebellion there had been a partial drought which had done considerable harm to the native crops; and, finally, came the outbreak of rinderpest which carried away over 100,000 head of cattle.

All these evils were ascribed to the bad influence of the white man, and were seized upon eagerly by the Witchdoctors as a means to incite the kraals to revolt. Further, there was one matter which was causing deep and legitimate discontent. Subsequent to the first confiscation of cattle by the Chartered Co. after the war of '93, there had been a periodical seizure of small numbers from the native herds. All the animals in the country – about 90,000, had been branded with the Company's brand and left with the natives to look after. It was understood that the Company would take from time to time such cattle as they required, but at the same time the promise was made that only animals which had belonged to the King would be confiscated, those belonging to private owners remaining in the herds of their masters. When the promise was given the authorities acted under the belief that nearly all the cattle in

Matabeleland had belonged to the King, and that the private owners had been but a small body of men; but they were undoubtedly mistaken, for every man of standing in the country had been a cattle owner, some of the more important indunas possessing enormous herds. But the Native Commissioners, when receiving orders to send to Bulawayo without delay certain numbers of cattle from their districts, could never have completed their work if they had listened to all the claims made to private ownership previous to the war – many of them false – and so they had to use their own discretion. Thus many natives suffered, the small cattle owners sometimes losing all they had, and the impression was formed that the promises of the white rulers were worthless. A settlement of the question was come to before the start of the rebellion, to the avowed satisfaction of the natives concerned, but the mischief had already been sown. There was a general feeling of distrust and unrest abroad which was constantly being aggravated by the tactless and tyrannical conduct of the native police, servants of the white administration, who, when sent to the kraals to see that the labour regulations were being carried out and the laws of the country generally adhered to, usually exceeded their duties and flaunted their little authority in the tyrannical manner beloved of the native mind. But the chief grievance of all was the loss of the independence of the Matabele. They – a proud and warlike people – had only been permitted to return to their own country, whence they were driven during the first war, under certain conditions which still rankled in the minds of men who three years ago had been a nation of rulers. Every young man had to work for a certain number of months each year at a fixed rate of pay, and each year the labour regulations grew more and more irksome to the people who represented one of the most indolent of all the races of the world. In fact, civilisation, with its blessings and its more noticeable burdens, had been tried by the savage Matabele for three years and found wanting. Mr. Selous, in his excellent book on the campaign of '96, has given us a capital illustration of the mental state of the insurgents in the following words, which are supposed to emanate from the lips of a black politician: 'Hang your Pax Britannica, give me the good old times of superstition; then, even if I did not know the day or the hour when I might be "smelt out" as a witch, and forthwith knocked on the head, at any rate I could have basked in the sun until my end came; and then, too, when the impi went forth, what glorious times I had, and how I revelled in blood and loot'. The little that historians have gleaned from the secret history of the rebellion makes it obvious that the rebel leaders must, a long time back, have determined to rise whenever opportunity occurred. They were fully prepared for action when the M.M.P. left for Johannesburg, though at first the revolt was not general. For a fighting force, they possessed some 17,000 able-bodied men, with muzzle-loading guns of every description, and about 2,000 breech-loading rifles. They had a large and well distributed supply of ammunition and every impi that engaged in the campaign showed itself to be well furnished, especially with Martini-Henry cartridges.

On the other side, there was no organised force of Britishers in the country. It may be said that there was no native police at all, for on the commencement of hostilities half of them went over to the enemy with their arms and equipment, while the other half who remained loyal had to be disbanded, for fear of accidents. Of the Mounted Police there remained forty-eight officers, non-commissioned officers and men in the whole of Matabeleland, under Inspector Southey. Of these, twenty-two were stationed in Bulawayo, and the rest at Gwelo, Selukwe, Belingwe, Inyati, Mangwe, Tuli, Matopos, Mzingwane, and Iron Mine Hill. When the rebellion broke out only twelve of these men were available at Bulawayo for immediate service and these, under Inspector Southey, accompanied Mr. Gifford's patrol to Insiza. Five hundred of the Rhodesia Horse were soon mustered in Bulawayo, but most of them could not be called upon except for the defence of the town, owing to the lack of horses, of which they only had 62. The Britishers in the province had a total 580 rifles all told, with an additional 80 old Martini-Henrys, more or less serviceable. Of ammunition, there was the good supply of 1,500,000 rounds. In Bulawayo, there was one serviceable Maxim, two 2.5 screw guns (with only 17 rounds between them), one Hotchkiss, one Gatling, one Gardner, one Nordenfeldt, and one seven-pounder. There were a further two old Maxims and two seven-pounders, but these were unserviceable during a large part of the campaign, one of the seven pounders being without a carriage and the two Maxims being also out of repair.

It will be seen that the position was a very serious one, and, had a little more generalship and common sense been exhibited by the insurgent leaders, it is probable that the white inhabitants of Rhodesia would have been massacred to a man before outside help could be obtained. Fortunately, there seemed to be no concerted plan of action on the part of the impis; the warriors appearing to trust entirely to the belief that the 'M'limo', The First Murder or God, would send down his supernatural powers to their aid.

The first open act of rebellion consisted of the murder of a native on the night of the 20th March. A party of eight native policemen had arrived on patrol at Umgorshlwini, a place situated in the hills near the Mzingwane River. They were accompanied by several boys who carried their blankets and patrol equipment, and together they formed quite a large party. After their evening meal, as they sat talking over their fires, a number of Matabele from the neighbouring kraal lined up in front of them and commenced to dance. It grew evident that they had come to pick a quarrel. As they danced they sang to the representatives of the law these words: 'You are killing us, you are killing us; why don't you cut our throats, and make an end of it? Why don't you shoot us?'

The police sergeant told Mzobo, the induna, to take his men away as nobody wanted to fight with them. Almost at once there came a sudden attack from a native who had crept up with an assegai in his hand. He was seized by two of the Police, when a shot was fired, from the shelter of the cattle kraal, which went wide, killing the captive. The 'Black Watch' party stood by their fires, irresolute for a moment, when a volley was directed against them from the bush near by. None of the police were hit, but one of the blanket-carriers was shot through the head and killed on the spot. Another boy of ten or twelve years of age, also attached to the party, was captured by the rebels during the retreat, and murdered in a most brutal way, his skull being smashed to atoms with knobkerries. The rest reached home in safety.

CHAPTER SIXTEEN

'Let us do Some More Killing' – 'Little England' and Mr. Labouchere's Sorrow – Gifford's Patrol

The natives at Umgorshlwini were by this time well blooded, and the night was not to pass without yet another tragedy. After the retreat of the police, one of Umyobo's men, Ganyamba, proceeded to the kraal of Umfondisi, a nephew of Lobengula. There he related what had occurred, crying out excitedly: 'Come, Umfondisi, why are you sleeping? Don't you know we're fighting? We've killed some policemen! Come, blood is running and men are lying dead! Come with me and let us do some more killing.' The two then hastened to a neighbouring kraal, where another native policeman happened to be passing the night. He was asleep when they arrived but, being awakened by the tumult they were causing at the kraal, he came out from his hut, asking what all the noise was about. 'Who are you?' said Ganyama. 'So and so, a policeman,' was the answer. 'What!' Rejoined Ganyamba, 'you dare to say you are one of the witches that has given us so much trouble?' and running up close he shot him, the king's nephew following the act with an assegai thrust as he lay mortally wounded.

The first step had been taken. Now the Matabele had no further hesitation. They began, quite openly, to sharpen their axes and gather together their shields, assegais, and guns, with the white ox-tail decorations and the other paraphernalia they had been accustomed to use in their old wars. On Monday the 23rd, Mr. Bentley, a Native Commissioner, with six other whites and their native servants, were murdered at and about Edkin's store, near the southern border of the Essexvale district. On the same day the massacre of the whites was commenced in the Insiza district, the first victims being the Cunningham family, who were living on a farm near the Insiza river, and Mr. Maddocks, the manager of the Nellie Reef Mine. In a very short space of time the trouble spread as a well organised rebellion from the Umzingwani through Filabusi and Insiza, to the Shangani and thence to the mining camps in the neighbourhood of Gwelo, embracing as a matter of fact every part of Matabeleland where men and children could be surprised and murdered, singly or in small parties. By the evening of the 30th not a white man was left alive in the outlying districts, though some had escaped or been brought into Bulawayo by relief parties. These dastardly murders, perpetrated frequently on defenceless women and children, excited a natural desire for a bloodthirsty vengeance in the hearts of every real man in the country, whether policeman or volunteer, and, to the everlasting credit of Rhodesian manhood, the whole available white population had formed itself into a keen and, more or less, efficient army in little over a day on hearing the tidings of brutality and rapine, and so could be classed in one or other of these categories. The one feeling that had come to every man was a burning and rightful lust for active personal participation in the killing of the murderers. Henceforth, no more quarter was asked for or given on the part of the British than had been given by the inhuman wretches that had rebelled, and one more delightful opportunity for slander and meanness, of the highest kind, was afforded to the gang of 'Little Englanders,' with Mr. Labouchere of 'Truth' at their head, that had tried in vain to crush the growth of young Rhodesia from the earliest days of her stormy infancy. Labouchere heaped the most infamous calumnies his pen could contrive on the heads of the gallant settlers, hinting that they were assassins of the worst type and that the 'poor' natives were angels of God in comparison. His only reference to the shattered brains of his dead countrywomen, and the dismembered limbs of the frail and innocent little children that had been so foully murdered, in many cases after most horrible torture, lay in a profession that he was 'sorry for the women and children who have been killed.'

There was no time in Rhodesia for retaliation, however. The authorities in Bulawayo had no difficulty at all in finding men who were ready to supplement the small handful of M.M.P. that had been left in the territory and proceed at once to the relief of the people in the outlying districts. Three little columns were dispatched within a few hours of the time when the first alarm was given. The Hon. Maurice Gifford was the first to leave. He took with him forty men, twelve of whom were police, under Capt. Southey, the object of the patrol being the relief of a party which had gone into laager at Cummings' store on the Insiza.

About twenty-six miles from Bulawayo, the column came across the first visible sign of the rising. An abandoned wagon was found by the roadside, with the sixteen donkeys lying dead, and the cargo of provisions on the wagon untouched. The Cape Boys in charge, as was afterwards discovered, had been murdered in the bush some little distance away.

On Thursday night, March 26th, the column reached Cumming's store, when they found about 30 men in laager. Many of these were unarmed, so that Gifford had only about 50 rifles, all told, at his command. There was no disturbance that night, but at 5 a.m. next morning, one hour before sunrise, about three hundred warriors rushed in with all the terrifying shouts and all the pluck of their Zulu forefathers. One of them was killed with his hands on the windowsill of the store, while three were shot alongside the walls of one barricade, and three more within a very short distance. On the British side, Sgt.-Major O'Leary of the Police fell together with an educated American negro, while six white men were wounded. As soon as the attack was beaten off, the wagons were inspanned, the laager was broken and the hazardous retreat to Bulawayo was commenced. The first portion of the road lay amongst broken, wooded kopjes, through which it was expected the column would have to fight every inch of the way, but though the Matabele assembled on some of the hills overlooking them they refrained from further attack, and so the whites were enabled to reach the open country where they were comparatively safe. But one of the wounded Policemen, Cpl. Strutt, lay in a critical situation, and shortly afterwards he died.

CHAPTER SEVENTEEN

The Attempted Relief of Mr. Graham – Last Stand of the Inyati Police – Panic in Bulawayo

At Inyati, the Native Commissioner, Mr. Graham, had gone into laager with the two policemen who, at the time, garrisoned the district, Lieut. Mark Handley and Tpr. George Case with two ex-members of the M.M.P, Leighton Huntley Corke, and George Hurford, and the miners, Patrick Madden and Tim Donovan, with their Cape servant. A multitude volunteered to go out to their relief immediately on the receipt of the news in Bulawayo; but as the Government were unable to furnish them with horses and rifles, only those could go who were in a position to equip themselves. Mr. Moodie Thompson, the editor of the *Matabele Times*, who accompanied the expedition, has left on record a most interesting account of the patrol, from which we have extracted the following:-

The kopjes in which we had expected to have trouble were passed, and the more open undulating ground at the Elibaini Hills reached. Progress was slow along this ascending road, and near the highest point skirting the base of the most prominent hill a strip of bush was entered. No sooner had we made our way into this cover than a shot was heard from the hill slope. In a second it was seen to be occupied by half-a-dozen or so natives, who sent in another and another shot. It was impossible to make a sufficient reply from our position, and a dash was made from the road through the strip of bush to the open slope of the hill. One or more of the natives was shot as they retreated over the crest, and a hot pursuit was made.

When those of our party who were foremost reached the top of the hill they found that affairs assumed a different aspect from repulsing a handful of stray rebels. A glance was sufficient. The natives were there in a dense mass, throwing skirmishers on either flank to surround us, one body proceeding rapidly along the lower slope to cut us off. Our advance men fell back, and the natives began to show themselves in the open. Firing became hot on both sides, but taking advantage of the strip of bush we were able at first to inflict considerable damage. The natives to the number of about three hundred were soon in the bush also, advancing in excellent open order and becoming formidable. Several rushed in to close quarters and Capt. Pittendrigh, who had dismounted, lost his horse. Before he could get one of the spare horses, a native armed with an assegai grappled him, and a hand-to-hand struggle took place. The native, however, was thrown off and shot, and the captain escaped with some slits in his coat. At the same moment, Thomas Aaden, who had been fighting most determinedly in the front, received a shot on the upper part of his bandolier, which exploded three of his cartridges, one bullet passing through his shoulder and with a ricochet entering his neck and passing through his cheek. Immediately after, Mr. S. Carter received a bullet through his ankle. The natives began to approach closer in their attack despite our heavy fire, and as they were gradually surrounding us, it was found advisable, encumbered as we were with two wounded men, to retire to the road.

With a rush through without further casualty on our side, we regained the road and found that one of our boys at the mule wagon had vanished, and the other was getting away on one of the spare horses. The mules and cart had therefore to be abandoned, and at a good pace we cut across through the lower bush over rough ground, avoiding the curve round the hills, to where it bent round in the open.

Here half-sections were again formed, the wounded in front, and a quick canter gave us a good start. Looking back, the natives could be seen in hot pursuit, and it was thought they might be able to reach one of the kopjes ahead, whose base we must skirt. Suggestions as to taking up a position on a kopje were untenable on account of the wounded men, and there was nothing for it but to get over the seventeen miles to the Bembesi as rapidly as possible. Again and again the natives seemed to be closing up on us, and sundry indications were closely scrutinised as to the presence of hostile forces ahead. The ride was made heavier by two of the ponies becoming done up. It was an anxious time, as the road ran through the hollows, but the clearness of the day gave abundant scope for noting the absence of an enemy ahead and the black mass falling farther astern.

About eleven o'clock Campbell's Store came in sight, and we crossed the Bembesi with gladdened spirits. These, however, were immediately damped. The news was awaiting us that the party at Inyati, eight miles farther on, which we had been sent to relieve, had been massacred. The intelligence was given by Patrick Madden, miner, who, and a native in his employ were the sole survivors. This man told with most circumstantial and convincing detail how Native Commissioner Graham, Inspector Handley, George Hurford, George Case, and L.H. Corke had fought against ever increasing odds on the evening of the previous Friday, this was now Sunday, until they were killed. Madden, another miner named Tim Donovan, and a colonial native had made for the hills, and after two day's hiding Madden and the native had reached this store.

This murder had been committed on March 26th. The little band of whites had set out from the shelter of the police camp at Inyati with a wagon, proceeding towards Bulawayo. They had not travelled a mile when they were attacked by a large force of natives, part of an impi of from 1,200 to 1,500 men, who had assembled in the neighbourhood. Mr. Graham and his companions had defended the wagon with the coolness and courage that had been displayed by Allan Wilson in '93, in the famous fight on the Shangani. They had battled on grimly, though without a shadow of hope, until every cartridge was exhausted and they could only stand proudly to meet the fatal thrust. Eighty-five empty cartridge cases were afterwards picked up around their dead bodies.

All this time the position of the settlers throughout Rhodesia was becoming more and more desperate. Even in Bulawayo itself, despite the comparatively large numbers of town population, the citizens grew nervier every day. Things were brought to a head on March 26th when some individual accidentally fired a rifle in the suburbs. Immediately the 'Alarm' and 'Double' were sounded repeatedly by the buglers inside the town. A panic ensued. The women and children were huddled without any sort of ceremony into the Club building, which had just been erected. Undisciplined throngs of the men rushed about aimlessly, not knowing what to do or where their services might be of use. Rifles were issued in frantic haste by the authorities, with disastrous results. Many gallant warriors found themselves in the possession of serviceable Lee-Metford rifles, but no other cartridges than those to fit the large bore Martini. Some of the people who had been lucky enough to receive the right things had never handled guns in their lives, and at least one stalwart was seen in the streets endeavouring to ram a cartridge down the muzzle of his rifle. Another asked with a quiver in his voice if it was safe to carry cartridges in his hand.

Surely, he suggested, that they would go off in the heat that Bulawayo was enduring at the time.

CHAPTER EIGHTEEN

Some Laager Prices
– The Mission of Father Prestige, S.J.
– Disbandment of the Native Police
– The Company's Problem

The laager was to undergo further panics before settling down. On one occasion, some old dynamite charges, exploding in a well on the Market Square, gave the impression that the whole force of the impis of the Matabele had gathered round the town. Fortunately, the enemy had left open the coach road to the South in the hope that the whites would clear out in a body and so leave the territory, without further bloodshed, to its old possessors, and one result was that coach after coach came through loaded with such plentiful supplies of ammunition that the garrison had far more than it could ever need. But there was a serious lack of food for men and horses, and disease was rife. The following figures, taken at random from a list of laager prices, will show something of the privations that were suffered at the time:-

Eggs 74/- per dozen.
Cauliflower 32/6 each.
Milk 30/- per bottle.
Fowls 20/- each.
Potatoes £30 per bag.
Small bunches carrots, etc., 1/- and 1/6 (about 5/- per lb.)

The general state of tension was much relieved by the good result of the labours of the Jesuit Father Prestige and the disbanding of the native Police. Father Prestige, whose tact and knowledge of the savage mind had always secured for him great influence among the natives, went out from the laager alone into the hill districts around Bulawayo. There he demanded personal interviews with the turbulent and the wavering chieftains, and not only did he succeed in bringing in several of the wiser indunas, thus removing them from the reach of their insurgent brethren, but he also persuaded some of the more reckless of the leaders to make peace and keep it. About this time it was seen that while many of the Native Police in Matabeleland had remained and were likely to stay loyal, so many had gone over with their arms to the Matabele, and so many were doubtful in their sympathies, that it was necessary to disband the whole regiment. 126 of the Native Police had proved their loyalty, but no less than 172 had openly joined the other side, and 32 were doubtful. Even in headquarters, 15 out of 60 were doubtful, while in the Bulawayo districts the loyalists and rebels were equally divided. In Bulalima and Gwanda practically the whole lot stood by the colours, while the rebels were in a large majority in Umzingwani, Mangwe, and Nsiza; and in Belingwe, Gwelo, and Bubi there was only one boy who had elected to continue in his duties. Several of the 'Black Watch,' of course, had been killed by the insurgents on the outbreak of the rebellion.

The attitude of many of these native policemen gives a curious insight into the effect of discipline on the native mind. For instance, the first warnings to reach Belingwe came from a black policeman, who had been dispatched by Mr. Fynn, the N.C. of the Insiza district. This boy, through whose services probably the whole of the whites in the Belingwe district escaped with their lives, faithfully carried out his duty in the face of the gravest danger, knowing all the while that if he fell into the hands of the rebels he would meet with probable torture and certain death. Yet, on the conclusion of his mission, it is known that he never returned to duty but went over to the insurgents with his rifle and a bandolier full of cartridges.

On March 30th, Inspector Southey, with a strong force of 60 men, Police and others, was sent out along the Tuli Road to act as escort for a coach that was coming through. No opposition was encountered, and the patrol returned at midnight. On the same day, a Police trooper, Bowker by name, was murdered while on his way to warn some outside people at Lower Gwelo.

By the middle of April, Bulawayo held some 1,500 white men, women and children who, while they were able to visit their houses in different parts of the town by day, had to seek the safety of the laager each night, and were not allowed to leave before seven o'clock in the morning. The whole of Matabeleland, with the exception of Bulawayo, and the laagers of Gwelo and Belingwe, was in the hands of the Kaffirs, although by the orders of the Umlimo the road to the south had been left open.

A large impi lay at Redbank, on the Khami river, about twelve miles to the west of the town, while some thousands of rebels headed by Lobengula's eldest son, Inyamanda, were camped along the Umguza, large numbers of them being actually within three miles of Bulawayo, and two other big impis had taken up their quarters among the Elibaini Hills and in the neighbourhood of Thabas Induna. There were no less than 10,000 well armed insurgents spread out in a semi-circle from the west to the north-east of the town. Had they only acted in concert, under one leader, the whites would probably have been wiped out to a man, but each impi was acting independently of the others in the expectation of some supernatural interference on their behalf. Besides the impis to the north and west, there were others scattered within the edge of the Matopos, but although they blocked the Tuli Road, they never attempted to approach the town.

The problem which lay before the Company was how to send food supplies, forage, arms, ammunition, and reinforcements to a population of over 4,000 in a town 587 miles away from its railway base, and besieged by an enemy numbering over 15,000 fighting men. The rinderpest had destroyed the main sources of meat and milk supply on which the town had depended for its food, also the transport by which the requirements of the population had been served; mules, which must be fed with a constant supply of grain, had to be organised at a moment's notice in place of the old ox transport. Owing to the famine not one single feed of corn could be obtained along the whole length of road stretching from Mafeking to Bulawayo. The extent of the transport difficulties will be realised when it is understood that ox wagons will carry from 8 to 9,000lbs with the necessity of forage for the oxen, a mule will only carry from 4 to 5,000lbs (*sic*), and mules, to keep their condition, must be fed at a minimum rate of 6lbs. of grain per day. A mule wagon train of 14 mules should receive a minimum 84lbs a day, or 2,520lbs of grain on a journey of 30 days, which was the time taken by wagons from Mafeking to Bulawayo along the Sumokwe at the average rate of 20 miles a day.

CHAPTER NINETEEN

Lieut. Chesnaye's Escape – The Second Phase of the Rebellion – Dr. Jim's Police to the Rescue

A story typical of many that were being made in the outside districts during the progress of the laager is told by Lieut. Chesnaye of the Police. The tale is related here in his own words:-

It was during the end of March when a number of us were at the Que Que Store, that we received a summons from a trooper in the M.M.P., who warned us that an outbreak of the natives was imminent. A similar warning was given to the prospectors and miners at the Sebakwe mine, who, acting upon it, trekked into our camp. Captain Pocock had in the meantime arrived, and I asked him if in his opinion the report was true, whether it was merely a local affair or a general rising, with the result that we came to the conclusion that there was nothing to cause serious alarm. We had about fourteen boys in the camp at the time and, seeing that there was no uneasiness amongst them, thought it was just a scare. That night however, thinking it was best to be on the safe side, we started towards Gwelo. On the way Pocock and myself decided to call at Harbord's Store, Ingwenia, hoping to find a goodly number of prospectors collected at that place, when, if things were as black as they painted, we could either proceed altogether to Gwelo, or else make a stand at the store.

We arrived there at dusk, and, on going into the store, asked for Harbord, who, we were told, had already left for Gwelo. We sat there until half past ten, talking and generally discussing the position of affairs, quite forgetting that if the rebellion were a fact we were in a most precarious situation. Suddenly the silence outside was broken by a shout and a yell, and in rushed, as well as we could judge, about half a score of natives, armed with assegais. The foremost of these made a lunge at Pocock, striking him on the shoulder, but at such an angle that it glanced off. Walker, who was standing behind the counter, took up a bottle, the first weapon of defence handy, and directed a blow at the assailants with it. They, seeing a flash in the dim candlelight, probably imagined it to be an arm of some description and, recoiling suddenly, knocked the assegai out of the hand of the native who stabbed Pocock, then the whole gang seemed to be seized with panic, and fled into the open. We had a few rifles, but no ammunition. It then suddenly occurred to one of the party that a surveyor, named Fitzpatrick, who was working in the vicinity, might be in his tent. On rushing out to see, we could hear our would-be murderers shouting to each other in the mealie fields, and on reaching Fitzpatrick's tent, which was a little distance from the store, we found him lying on his bed, stabbed through the throat and heart.

In order to avoid the natives who, judging from their shouts, were on the Gwelo Road, our little band started in the only direction apparently open, and by making a detour of forty miles, which we covered in ten hours, eventually reached Gwelo in safety.

The news of the rising in Matabeleland had by this time created a stir of excitement throughout South Africa, and even to the aggressive portion among the Dutch population, the recent Jameson Raid became a matter of only secondary importance. It was generally felt that this was a case of White against Black, and both the White races were quick to show their proper appreciation of the position. Among the offers of gratuitous assistance made to the Chartered Co. were those of the officials of the Transvaal Republic, while Volunteer forces, British and Dutch, from all parts of the sub-continent, expressed their instant readiness to march to the assistance of their fellows in Rhodesia. The Company proceeded to enrol a relief column under the command of Major Plumer, of the York and Lancaster Regiment, which was to start at once for Bulawayo. The pay offered was 7/6 per day. Recruiting was commenced at Kimberley and Mafeking on April 6th, and with the exception of 150 men and 163 horses raised at Jo'burg, all recruiting was done at those two places. The original strength was to have been 500, but this was afterwards raised to 750, in order to include those members of the Company's police who had been sent to England on the conclusion of the Raid, and who were now on their way back.

The first troop left Mafeking on April 12th, and the others started as follows:-

No. 2 Troop – April 14th   No. 3 Troop – 15th
No. 4 Troop – 16th   No. 5 Troop – April 17th
No. 7 Troop – 19th   No. 8 & 9 Troop – 20th
Signallers and Medical Detachment: 21st
No. 10 Troop and Scouts with 50 horses: 23rd
Maxim Detachment: 24th
No. 11 Troop and d'mtd detachment: 25th
No. 12 Troop: 29th
No. 13 Troop: 30th
No. 14 Troop: May 1st

The last three troops, which constituted 'E' Squadron of the Matabeleland Relief Force, were composed almost entirely of the old Police who had taken part in the ill-fated march to Krugersdorp, and they were dispatched from Mafeking without further training immediately on their arrival from England. Capt. Drury commanded the squadron, while the troop leaders were Lieuts. Cazalet, Murray and Abbott. 'E' Squadron formed the rearguard for the column and left Macloutsie for Khami on May 24th (Queen's Birthday), the day the advanced troops had their first brush with the Matabele on the Umgusa. On reaching Shashi River, next day, Capt. Drury addressed his men. Over the river, he said, commenced the enemy's country. The squadron would in future march with advance and rear guards, and a flanking patrol on either side of the wagons. Laager would be formed each night, and he might remind them that anyone found asleep on guard was liable to be court-martialled. Shortly after this the squadron rejoined the rest of the column at Hope Fountain, on the Khami river, a day's march from Bulawayo.

On June 5th, the order was given to the whole column with the exception of 'B' Squadron to start on a twenty days' patrol down the Gwaai River. The force left camp 450 strong, with three Maxims and sixteen transport wagons.

CHAPTER TWENTY

The Gwaai Patrol – Sergeant-Major Blatherwick's Adventure – The Failure of the Commissariat – Hi-Tiddly-Hi-Ti-Who Goes There – The Colonel's Bath

News had been received that a number of impis had assembled in some villages to the north of the Khami Drift. Going in pursuit of these, the Column reached Mayesa's Kraal on June 7th but found it deserted. The scouts were sent to discover the whereabouts of the impi, but without success, although from the signs of fresh spoor in every direction it was evident that they were lurking in force no great distance away. Afterwards indeed, it was ascertained from some prisoners who had been captured that an impi of several thousand warriors had been within four miles of the spot where the scouts camped for the night, and it was by the merest chance that they was not wiped out.

On June 8th, a troop from 'A' Squadron, under Lieut. Cashel, surprised a small party of the enemy. As the incident nearly resulted in the death of the fine soldier who is to-day the regimental sergeant-major of the B.S.A.P.-R.S.M. Blatherwick, it will be worth while to give an account of the affair in full in the words of the officer in charge of the patrol:-

> On the day in question I was ordered to patrol near the Khami River, supposed to be about 15 mile north of the column. I went about 10 miles and burned several kraals, coming across the spoor of some natives in the bush. As the country became very thick I gave the order to return. When about half a mile on the way back, and as we were rounding the corner of a clump of bush, we came on a party of rebels in front of us. I saw five but there were more in a kraal about 500 yards to the right of our advance.
>
> Sending a sergeant and half my party over to the kraal, with the remainder I pursued the rebels we had first seen, and who were now running away. On seeing us in pursuit, they scattered. Drawing my revolver, I singled out one

and followed him. On my approach he lay down his rifle, and I lowered my revolver as he did so. No sooner, however, had he noticed this action on my part, then up come his rifle within a foot of my chest. I instantly fired, shooting him through the heart, and sent another bullet through his head to make sure. How it was he failed to shoot first is a mystery; either his gun must have misfired, or in the confusion of the moment he must have failed to find the trigger. Anyhow, it was to be the one or the other of us, and fortunately, to use an American expression, 'I got the bulge on him.' While this was going on, Sergeant-Major Blatherwick was being engaged singlehanded with some of the enemy. Seeing this, I galloped up to him.

Blatherwick, covering one of his opponents with his revolver, pulled the trigger, but the cartridge misfired. The next moment his intended victim hurled his assegai at the Sergeant-Major, striking him in the lower part of the back as he rode past. The latter was quickly avenged however, for almost at the same moment I dropped the fellow with a shot at close quarters. Of the remainder, two were killed and the other was taken prisoner. The natives of the kraals made good their escape into the thick bush before my men could get amongst them.

The patrol met with but little further incident, save for the burning of the villages. The line of march was marked by a long succession of blazing kraals numbering some hundreds. The enemy could not be found in force, he had either retreated to the hills or, what is more probable, evaded the column on its approach.

The commissariat was as poor as it well could have been. In a surprisingly short time the men were put upon half rations. These, besides being small in quantity, were almost unfit to eat, and reflected the utmost discredit on those whose duty it was to look after the welfare of the troops.

But what little was doled out day by day had to be made the most of and, as rice, meal, fat, and baking-powder were obtainable, bread became almost the staple food of the campaigners. On the return of the column to Khami Fort, a store wagon, stocked with tobacco and other luxuries was found. This had been brought from Bulawayo by some enterprising person who charged his customers at the profit of 100 per cent on the cost in the town.

On the march, the lack of tobacco constituted a very real privation. All kinds of substitutes were experimented on. Some men took to the weird and wonderful native article after a time, as though they had smoked it all their lives, others tried dried Mopani leaf, but this was unanimously pronounced to be a failure. On many occasions half a crown was paid for a single cigarette, while one man made no less than £5 on twelve packets of 'Three-Castles' cigarettes. A half-pound cake of black tobacco fetched £2, while a handful of 'Mahaliesberg' was bought in by some lucky purchaser at 5/-. The customary ration of 'dop' was altogether absent from the patrol. As for the horses, overwork, underfeeding and horse-sickness were rampant, and an enormous number of the animals perished. Twenty-five percent of the transport mules were lost with them. In consequence hosts of the less fortunate troopers were reduced to the necessity of 'foot-slogging' in the rear of the wagons, and as the soil of the Gwaai district is in most places as good a sample of apparently bottomless Rhodesian sand as can be found, their language may easily be imagined by the present day trooper, to whom many of the choice epithets of the old timer have been handed.

Another worry which the column had to undergo was caused by the 'meat and meal' diet, which caused even the hardiest campaigners to break out in veldt sores. The bodies of some of the men were covered with these loathsome eruptions. Again no lime juice had been provided to remedy this evil. This is said to have accounted for the high percentage of cases during the rebellion in which comparatively slight wounds terminated in the death of the sufferer.

The troops were so discontented with all these grievances that, on the conclusion of the patrol, about one sixth of them formally applied for their discharges from the Force. Colonel Plumer, however, refused to grant any discharges unless the applicant could show a certificate of medical unfitness, or any other urgent reason for departure. As he said on general parade each member of the Force had signed to serve for such a period as his services might be required, and there was still much to be done.

Although the column had seen no fighting to speak of on the patrol, they had been over a large tract of country in a comparatively short space of time, and had accomplished some good work. He did not under-estimate the hardships they had been called upon to undergo, or the amount of work and he was pleased at the readiness and good will with which the duties had been performed.

In spite of the grumbling, it seems evident, from the unusual amount of picket yarns of the patrol that have been recorded, that the men were on the whole a cheery lot, two of these stories are worth repeating here. On one occasion an orderly officer, going his rounds, was surprised to find himself challenged, or otherwise sung at, in this fashion: 'Hi tiddley hi ti. Who goes there?' He enquired of the songster the meaning of this extraordinary behaviour. The sentry replied that the last time he was on duty he had been told to give the challenge in a more musical voice, and that was the only tune he knew.

Whenever a prolonged halt was made, the available water was divided off into sections. One was for drinking purposes, one for the men to wash in, and one for the officers. A guard was posted, whose duty it was to see that no one mistook the drinking water for the washing pool, and that the men did not bathe in the place kept apart for the officers. One day the water-guard saw the naked figure of an elderly man climbing down to the officers' pool for a plunge. Thinking he recognised him as a man in his squadron, he shouted, 'You old ----------- come out of that, go and wash your dirty--------.' At that moment the bather turned his head disclosing, to the dismay of the sentry, the well known features of Colonel Plumer. Too frightened even to apologise, the hasty trooper took to his heels, leaving the gallant officer to enjoy his bath in peace.

91

1. Maxim Gun crew, Bechuanaland Border Police

2. Macloutsie Camp Govt. Archives, Salisbury

3. Police Tents, Tuli Govt. Archives, Salisbury

4. Matabele Envoys at Tuli Govt. Archives, Salisbury

5. Officers of the B.S.A. Company Police, 1890 Govt. Archives, Salisbury
Left to right – Back Row (*standing*): Lieut. C.W.P. Slade, Dr. R.F. Rand.
Middle Row (*sitting*): Lieut. S.W.B. Shepstone, Capt. P.W. Forbes,
Lieut. Col. E.G. Pennefather, Lieut. M.D. Graham, Canon Balfour.
Front Row: Lieut. the Hon. E.W. Fiennes, Capt. H.M. Heyman.

6. Fort Salisbury Camp Govt. Archives, Salisbury

93

7. The capture of the Portuguese Camp in the valley below Umtassa's Kraal by the B.S.A. Co. Police. 1890

8. 'C' Troop, Salisbury Column about to leave for Matabeleland, 5 September 1893

9. Capt. Lendy and the Fort Victoria Police with Maxim Gun, 1893 Govt. Archives, Salisbury

10. Khama's Levies Govt. Archives, Salisbury

11. Dec. 15 1893. Maxim gun in action against Matabele

12. On parade at Fort Victoria Courthouse before riding out to attack the Matabele, 1893

13. The Victoria Rangers
Back; Stoddart, Hofmeyer, Bastard, Harris, Chalk, Fitzgerald, Kennelly, Molyneux,
  Bowden, Sampson
Middle; Judd, Lendy, Allan Wilson, Rixon, Hamilton
Front; Ware, Vaughan Williams , Swan (?) Greenfield, Beal
(Killed at Shangani; Hofmeyer, Fitzgerald, Judd, Wilson, Greenfield)

14. Capt. P.W. Forbes and Staff, Bulawayo 1893

15. Khami River Fort – the Look-Out Govt. Archives, Salisbury

16. Dr. Jameson and party leaving Pretoria gaol, 1896

17. Malema Camp, Matopos, Gen. Sir Frederick Carrington's base

18. Native Police under Capt. Harding, 1897 Govt. Archives, Salisbury

19. Bulawayo Laager Govt. Archives, Salisbury

20. Officers of Mounted Infantry
(*Sitting*) Major Godley, Lt. Col. Alderson

99

21 Mountain Screw Gun on parade; Matabeleland Division, BSAP 1898
On right is Batt. Sgt.Major Harris and Sgt Giles

22. Mashonaland Division, B.S.A.P. Artillery Troop 1898
Batt.Sgt.Major Harris on left.

23 B.S.A.P. Squadron on parade at Bulawayo prior to departure for active
service, 1900

24. Maxim gun company of Australian and New Zealand Imperial Bushmen accompanying Plumer's last advance to join up with Mahon.

25. B.S.A.P. Post, Col. Hore's headquarters, temporarily captured by Eloff

26. Heliographing from Limestone Fort to Cannon Kopje. The wheels of the 7-pounder are padded for moving at night.

CHAPTER TWENTY ONE

Inspection by General Carrington – Rhodes and the Trooper – 'Sitting on' the Bully – The Adventures of a Convoy – Thabas Amamba

On July 28th, the column was inspected by Sir Frederick Carrington, who had arrived to take over the command of the Army. He made a brief speech and recognised many of the Police Squadron, M.R.F., as men who had served with him before in his African campaigns. On the conclusion of the inspection, after a rest of only three days, the whole force was marched off once more towards Thabas Amamba, where the Matabele massed in large numbers. The objective of the British was to dislodge the enemy from the hills which lay beyond Inyati, and if possible to bring them to a decisive action in the open country. On the second day our reinforcements arrived, including the Bulawayo Squadron of the M.M.P.

Rations for 20 days were carried, 200 rounds of ammunition per man, and a large reserve for all arms. A section of No. 10 Mountain Battery, R.A., from Natal with 2.5 inch screw guns, accompanied the column. The numerical strength of the whole was about 1200, by far the largest of any column yet concentrated in Rhodesia. On the march it extended for close on a mile. The discipline of the troops was by this time excellent, and so perfect was the organisation that many of the troopers have recorded the surprise they felt discovering that the conditions of life can as comfortable for a unit of one thousand as for one of only fifty.

On June 29th, the Welsh Harp, on the Umguza River was reached and a days' halt was called. Here an amusing incident occurred. A hawker's wagon containing much needed supplies of tobacco and mess extras had been expected, and when a well stocked mule wagon rounded a bend in the road and came in sight of the men, a certain trooper, anxious to make sure that he had something to smoke on the march, ran from the laager to meet it. On nearing it, he unceremoniously commanded the driver to pull up. The wagon stopped and a head appeared from inside the cover, 'What have you got?' demanded the trooper. 'Who is this man?' muttered the occupant of the wagon. 'Look here,' continued the warrior, 'Have you any soap, matches, tobacco or candles?' The stranger gave a polite negative to the queries, whereupon the trooper gave his opinion of him in language that was more forcible than polite. 'You,' he said, 'You're a nice sort you are, I don't think, no soap. What the blankety blank blank did you come out here for?' A satisfactory answer to the question would probably have taken quite a time to deliver, for the owner of the head happened to be Cecil Rhodes himself, who was on his way to the scene of action to learn how the operations were progressing.

Further privations were in store for the troops. It was soon found that a large percentage of the bully beef rations was unfit for food. The consignment was part of a quantity that had been stored at Tuli where the cases had been used in constructing the walls of the fort. Having been submitted to much rough handling in the process, many of the tins were damaged and admitted air, whereby the meat was rendered unwholesome and possibly poisonous. On the discovery of this state of affairs, a Committee of Investigation, consisting of Col. Plumer, Major Bodle and Capt. Scott Turner, was formed and proceeded to sit on 'the beef' daily. Tins for the day's use were opened in their presence, and it was their duty to decide by test of smell whether the meat was passable or otherwise, every tin with the slightest suspicion of taint being at once cast aside. This duty was no sinecure, as there were between 300 and 400 tins to be inspected each day. Occasionally the troops were served out with Weil's 'road rations' which consisted of good beef, mutton and vegetables, and which were much coveted by the men. They were less economical, however, and so were not often issued. The supplies of sugar soon became exhausted, but some of the more fortunate troopers succeeded in looting the kraals for 'imfi' or native sugar cane, while one or two had even had the forethought to provide themselves with saccharine tablets, which proved to be most invaluable.

The column arrived at Inyati, the base for the attack on Thabas Amamba, on July 2nd. The main body proceeded to the scene of action during the night. The ambulance and transport wagons, together with a convoy of thirty-five men of the Police Squadron, M.R.F., and a tripod Maxim, under Lieut. Abbott, left Inyati at 2 a.m. the following morning, with instructions to join their comrades at the place of attack at daybreak. It was pitch dark when the convoy started and, as the escort spread over the veldt in extended order, many of the troopers came to grief among the meercat holes. The wagons travelled at a brisk trot and the flanking patrols experienced the greatest difficulty in keeping in touch with them amongst the rocks and bushes. At one moment an unfortunate trooper would find himself and his horse being lacerated by the cruel thorns of the wach-enbeetje bush, only to find release in the miniature inferno of an outcrop of granite boulders. However, in about three hours and a half, the cold light of dawn began to spread, but the country became still rougher, and the progress of the convoy slower.

Suddenly rifle shots and the booming of the big guns announced heavy fighting ahead. The convoy dashed forward, crossing a steep drift, and at last arrived at the base of Thabas Amamba. The column was not to be seen, but the sounds of firing in the hills, in every direction, showed that various detachments were not idle. Abbott laagered his wagons, set up the Maxim, and paraded twelve men for Cossack post duty. Two posts were stationed on some rocks overlooking the laager, and two on the flat country behind. One of the men selected for the hill posts has related his experiences and, as they gave a most interesting picture of typical Rhodesian warfare, they are worth recalling here:-

> I was detailed, with two others, to keep watch from the heights on the right front of the laager, as we followed the steep track, winding upwards amongst the boulders and bushes, a shot close behind me and 'That's got him!' from Sgt.-Major Mallett, called our attention to the writhing figure of a native under a rock to the left. Lieut. Oakley administered the coup de grace with a revolver bullet, and on we went towards the top. Climbing then began. In a few minutes the summit was reached. There we were posted for the day, with instructions to hold the position in case of attack as long as possible and then retire on the laager. With this the officer and sergeant-major left us to our own devices. It was now about seven in the morning. Choosing a spot behind a slab of rock breast high, fairly isolated, and with almost precipitous approach on three sides, we sought cover and were able to take stock of the situation. Immediately in front, and behind us was a circular plateau fringed round with rocks and bushes,

these in turn gave way to a deep descent into the valley 600 or 700 feet below. Beyond, to the right and in front, the eye travelled over a vast expanse of wild broken country, of hills upon hills, with sides more or less covered with bush, according to the abruptness of their declivity, each topped with giant obelisks, columns, and turret-shaped masses of granite, standing out clear and bold against the skyline. Here and there could be seen bold faces of smooth rock, rising up nearly vertically 200 or 300 feet, symmetrically rounded off towards the top, upon which rested immense blocks of stone, either solitary, and so the more conspicuous, or piled up in confused masses. It was a beautiful morning. A strong southerly breeze tempered the heat of the sun, and as one took in the full beauty of the surrounding scenery, it seemed hard to realise that the day and the place were being devoted entirely to the work of slaughter. As the rifle shots rang out from the valleys and slopes, now far away in the distance, now close at hand, one was strongly reminded of a day amongst the 'birds' at home; but in this case the beaters were Cape Boys, and the game human beings. Every now and again the weird howl or war cry of the hunted Kaffirs resounding amongst the rocks would be borne down the wind, and white puffs of smoke would be seen issuing here and there from the rocky crevices or from behind the boulders. Further away the heavy reports of the big guns came booming and reverberating through the kopjes, followed on by a continuous rattle of musketry, telling of some hot corner where the rebels were making a stand. Occasionally a herd of baboons, frightened out of their haunts by the unusual disturbance, would troop along the tops of the mountain range with slow and deliberate tread. Then one would leave the herd, and making his way cautiously to a prominent boulder, proceed to climb up slantwise, and having gained the summit gravely squat down, and from this coign of vantage attempt to discover what all the noise was about. Ungainly, awkward, and sullen as these brutes are, it was a revelation to see them clamber up an almost vertical face of rock with the greatest assurance and ease, and the hill natives, who have them for an example, are not much behind them in agility.

Once we fired some long-range shots at a rebel, but too far away to know whether they had taken effect. The noise of our shots brought up a small party from the laager, who thought we were being attacked. As the day wore on the firing got farther away, and we decided to have a prowl round amongst the rocks in our neighbourhood. Leaving one man at a post, we clambered down, and before we had gone thirty yards I noticed the colours of a blanket, deep down in a crevice of the rocks. A little farther on was an opening, with a sort of cave between the boulders. I followed it to the end, and there was the blanket jammed tightly in. On the ledge above were an assegai, battle-axe, and sandals. These I annexed, and was turning to go out, when a man behind me said, 'I'll have the blanket,' and started to pull at it. As he did so, up popped the head of a native, but before the latter could spring out Grant had him shot through the head. About a hundred yards farther on, beyond some large boulders, we came upon a number of boxes, travelling trunks, and tool-chests, all of which had been smashed open, and most of the contents taken. Lying around were a number of letters, Christmas and New Year cards (one of these had on it 'To dear Mother, from Ethel'), work-boxes, axe-heads, picks, and shovels. The Cape Boys had evidently been through this lot of effects, which no doubt had originally been looted by the Matabele from stores and houses in the vicinity. Taking with us a few mementoes of the place, we returned to our post, where we remained till after dark. As we made our way down to the laager, the lowing of cattle and the bleating of sheep and goats gave welcome assurance of a big haul, and soon we were discussing the events of the day and hearing the latest news from those who had been fighting among the hills.

At the laager an incident had occurred which might have terminated in a horrible tragedy. A large body of natives were seen approaching the wagon. The order to stand by was given by the officer in charge, but the natives continued to advance. Further delay would be dangerous, and Abbott was about to command his men to fire when it was seen that the crowd was composed entirely of women and children under the guard of a small party of Whites.

The dismounted men of the main column, 250 in all, had

stormed the long ridge of Thabas Amamba. 2,000 of the enemy had gathered on the mountain top, and the fight had raged steadily from early morning until two o'clock in the afternoon. Driven out by the mountain guns and the bayonets of Major Robertson's corps of Cape Boys, the natives had sought shelter in the hill caves, only to be smoked out and shot down as they emerged. The gallantry of the Cape Boys' corps, who showed the military value of the hatred for the pure Black, that is traditional of their race, was extreme, and certainly constituted the prime factor of the victory. Of the British forces twenty-five men were killed and wounded. The enemy lost 200 killed and about the same number wounded. 1,000 head of oxen were captured, 2,200 goats and sheep, together with 400 women and a multitude of children.

Next day all the kopjes in the neighbourhood were carefully searched, but no traces of the rebels were to be discovered. They had made off towards the mountain fastness of the Matopos. On the return of the column to the Welsh Harp the members of the Bulawayo Field Force marched away to the town, where they were disbanded. The others made for the foot of the Matopos, where a base camp was formed, and preparations were made for the final rout of the insurgents.

CHAPTER TWENTY TWO

The Matopos – The Attack on Babayana's Stronghold
– Not so Easy as it Looked – John Grootboom
– On the White Man's Tactics – Laing's Graveyard

The Matopos Hills, where the rebels were making their final stand, were at that time a terra incognita, hardly penetrated by a single white man. They form a range of mountain groups extending for 120 miles, with an average breadth of about 25 miles. Their northern base lies about 15 miles S.E. of Bulawayo. The mountain groups enclose hundreds of fertile valleys, intersected by no less than six important tributaries of the Limpopo and the Gwaai. These valleys are approached through narrow defiles which are only practicable for pack animals, and are connected by a maze of mountain gorges and neks. The mountains, immense blocks of granite thrown together in Nature's most freakish mood, piled up and leaning against each other in the most absurd attitudes, rise sometimes to the height of 2,000 to 3,000 feet, and contain gloomy caverns of every sort and size. Hidden amidst the dense undergrowth that clothes the crevices between the boulders, there are thousands of winding footpaths, made by generations of natives.

On the elevated plateaux provided by the flat tops of many of the boulders the Matabele had constructed their strongholds. They had chosen one of the most difficult countries in the world for an attacking enemy to wage any sort of successful warfare. Their valleys were all well watered, and they had ample ground for the growing of sufficient crops to supply the whole Matabele race with grain, and to raise and feed any number of sheep and cattle. Game was plentiful, and they had no fears concerning their food supplies for some years.

On the night of Sunday, July 19th, the column under the personal command of General Carrington left the base camp for the hills, where they were to attack the stronghold of Babayana, the notorious old war councillor of the Matabele. The rebels were known to be there in force. The place lay some 10 miles away from the camp, and a night march with an attack at dawn was decided upon. The scouts, supported by native friendlies on either side preceded the column. They were the M.M.P. (dismounted), then 'A' and 'B' squadrons M.R.F., supported by the Cape Corps and Colenbrander's Native Contingent, the Maxims and Hotchkiss of the M.M.P., the Mountain Battery, R.A., the Maxims M.R.F., Lieut. Mathias' troop, and the Police Squadron of the M.R.F.

On coming into touch with the enemy the R.A. hurried into position and commenced to fire shot after shot in quick succession. Under cover of the guns Colenbrander's boys and the friendlies advanced in extended order. The enemy could be seen in large numbers clearing from the flat ground and disappearing behind the cover of the rocks.

At 7 a.m. the distant booming of a field gun was heard in the hills to the right. A column under Capt. Laing, consisting of 170 whites, 300 friendlies, a Nordenfeldt, a seven-pounder, and a Maxim had been sent from Figtree on the previous day, with instructions to effect a junction with Carrington's force in the hills. His guns announced to the larger force that he was heavily engaged. The firing apparently ceased at 11 a.m. and nothing further of Laing was heard that day.

Meanwhile a party of the M.M.P., supported on the left by the Cape Boys and the friendlies, had engaged in a hand-to-hand conflict with the rebels on the heights, whom they soon put to flight, while a force under Col. Sergeant (5th Rifle Brigade) attacked and forced the enemy's position on their left flanks. The Matabele were successively dislodged from three positions. The friendlies, during the short scrap, lost their heads completely, and were firing off their rifles in all directions as fast as they could load them. They were not only useless as allies, but they were also a considerable source of danger to the whites and the Cape Boys they had come to assist. After a time the M.M.P. artillery, two Maxims and a Hotchkiss, under Capt. Llewellyn, were brought into action, and opened fire from the valley below. The enemy was speedily driven from his caves and thickets, and fled over the hills towards the South.

The losses on the British side were one white sergeant killed, and three Cape Boys killed and four severely wounded, and a number of friendlies wounded. The enemy's loss has been given in native accounts as 10, and by some of the Britishers who fought in the engagement as 200, so that it is well nigh impossible now to come to any satisfactory conclusion on the matter. Babayana's flight however, showed that the conquest of the Matabele on his ground was not to be such a simple affair as some had anticipated. He had learnt something since the outbreak of the rebellion, and he was proving now that he had the sense to put his knowledge to the best advantage. He was no longer facing the fire of the deadly 'Sikwakwa' (Maxims) in the open. He had taken to advancing in skirmishing order and volley firing instead. He was using his sights these days in the proper manner, and making use of every little bit of cover, and had begun to realise that he got better results by shooting at the gunners rather than their shells. John Grootboom, the famous coloured scout who accompanied Cecil Rhodes in the final 'indaba' where peace was declared and who was one of the real heroes of the rebellion, has contrasted the Matabele methods with those of the white leaders, which did not meet with his approval at all. The 'column,' he said, 'would march into the hills and have a fight, and then at night go back to camp. That is not the way to fight the Matabele. You must sleep in the hills after the battle, and keep on following the enemy from one kopje to another, and kill so many that you break his heart. But instead of doing that, you go back to camp and the Matabele thinks that you have had enough of it. Soon the rebels collect together again, and are more confident than ever. The white men don't understand fighting among the rocks. They go out in the open and let the Matabele shoot and shoot, and down they fall. I saw one man walk out from behind a rock and as he did so a Matabele shot him through the head. But you don't see Col. "Baking Powder" (Baden-Powell) do that. If they want to shoot him, they must go after him and catch him where he hides. He knows better than to stand up to be shot at.'

While the fight with Babayana was progressing, Capt. Laing barely managed to save the column from annihilation. He had entered the hills on the afternoon of the 19th. After crossing a valley through which run the Molongwe and Malema Rivers, he had left Inugu Mountains to the right and advanced about a mile up a narrow gorge as the sun was setting. Here, on the spot that was to become known as 'Laing's Graveyard', he laagered up for the night. The pass through which he had come led through dense bush, on either side at a distance of fifty or sixty yards rose the kopjes, covered with stunted bush which gave ideal cover for an ambush.

The enemy had evidently watched the movement of the

column from the time it entered the hills and they must have chuckled in astonished delight when they saw the white man select the very spot for a bivouac that most obviously invited attack. During the night the guard reported that he had seen natives lurking among the rocks. At daybreak the rebels, who had collected in force during the night, opened fire on the laager on two sides. The Britishers dashed at once for their rifles, and throwing themselves flat on the ground behind their saddles, commenced firing. Almost on the instant the natives swept down from the heights in a wild rush, determined to crush the little force in one fierce charge. Some of them actually advanced to within a couple of paces of the laager, but the two machine guns and the seven-pounder were brought into action without delay, and poured a withering fire into the too-exultant warriors. Their progress was checked, and they fled in disorder for the shelter of rocks. But the friendlies, who were encamped about 50 yards to the right of the main laager, were demoralised by the first attack, and had made a rush for the laager, crossing the line of fire of their own allies and losing about 30 lives before the order to cease fire could be given.

The rebels clambered up the kopjes immediately above the laager, and began to fire, well under cover, from within twenty or thirty yards from the line of saddles. Corpl. Hall of the Belingwe Field Force and Troopers Bush and Bennett of the M.M.P. were killed instantly, all of them being shot through the head. Ten troopers were wounded more or less seriously, one of them dying three days later. A number of men had their hats and clothing pierced by bullets, and no less than eleven horses were left dead on the field. Some of the saddles, which served as shields for the firing line, were riddled with bullet holes.

Capt. Laing made up in phlegmatic courage what he had lacked in foresight. He coolly walked about under a heavy fire, giving instructions to his men and inspiring them with confidence, in spite of the awful odds that confronted them. At 11 a.m. he succeeded in making a move, and the column advanced two miles further along the valley, laagering in the open. That afternoon and early the following day the march through the hills was continued, but it was seen that the valleys all led away towards the south, and as there was no outlet in the desired direction, Laing decided to retire. The column emerged from the hills without further trouble in two treks. There they were met by a relief party, under Capt. Beresford, with ambulance wagons from Plumer's column, and the combined force marched together to the base camp.

The natives who had taken part in the fight at Laing's Graveyard stated afterwards that had the column gone further into the hills instead of retiring, Laing would have found that they had blocked up the two ends of a gorge which he must have entered, and so he would have met with the final disaster from which he could not possibly have extricated the column. As it was, a large impi had followed close on his heels during the retreat, with the intention of making another attack in the Inugu Gorge, but they had been too late, coming up only just in time to see the last of his wagons leave the gorge, and they were not sufficiently confident to risk a fight in the open country.

CHAPTER TWENTY THREE

Capt. Nicholson's Attempt at the Inugu Gorge
– Sikombo's – Gallantry of the Police Gunner
– Extending the British Empire on Jupiter
– The March on Umlugulu – Bushed
– The End of the Rebellion

Four days after Laing's reverse, a column under Capt. Nicholson (7th Hussars), the Commandant of the M.M.P., left the base camp for the 'Graveyard,' with the object of teaching the rebels in the neighbourhood a well deserved lesson. The force consisted of 250 mounted men, 200 Cape Boys, two field guns and two Maxims. Camping in the open on the night of the 24th, they marched into the hills at daybreak, following the road which Capt. Laing's Column had originally taken. On nearing the scene of the disaster, the troops were advanced in skirmishing order, with the intention of attacking the kopjes on either side of the Gorge, but it was soon seen that the enemy had found an impregnable position and meant to keep it. The guns were posted in the mouth of the Gorge, to cover the advance of the White men as they crossed the pass under the shelter of the trees, but they were soon answered by a raking cross fire from the invisible Matabele. Within two or three minutes, four men were shot down, and the Commander ordered a retirement on the laager. Meanwhile, the Cape Boys had similar bad luck in the endeavour to dislodge the insurgents from the right side of the Gorge. The rocky cover which sheltered the Matabele was without a flaw, and the assailants also had to retire on the laager, with a loss of two killed and four wounded. It was a relief to the whole column when, after seven hours marching through most difficult and dangerous country, the Base Camp was at last regained.

By this time the problem that confronted the British forces seemed a hopeless one. Two attempts had been made to drive the rebels from their strongholds, both of them resulting in failure. For every ten natives killed a loss of one White man had been incurred, and at its strongest Plumer's whole column consisted only of 500 against 5,000 wily and undaunted warriors. However, in spite of the heavy odds that faced them, the hearts of Plumer's Column were as sound as ever, and the men continued their work of clearing the outer hills, leaving the rebels a gradually dwindling space in which to reign supreme. The next move was to the Mitshabezi Valley, whence the Matabele were evicted without overmuch difficulty. For the following fortnight Sugar Bush Camp (the site of what is now known as Umlugulu Fort) was selected as a base for operations against the natives congregated in the district. The Camp faced the impressive peaks of the S.E. Matopos, where the largest impis were reported to be lying. At daybreak on Wednesday, Aug. 6th, the whole force, with the exception of 'B' Squadron, two Maxims and a field piece, left for an advance in strength into the hills. Plumer was making for the stronghold of Sikombo, one of the strongest of the insurgent chiefs. The artillery, supported by the dismounted detachments under Capt. Beresford, led the way and took up their position on a hill to the West of Sikombo's position at an early hour. Here they started to shell the place. At half-past nine the remainder of the column entered the valley, which they began to cover in half-sections at a gallop.

A flag signal from Capt. Beresford warned Plumer that the guns were surrounded and needed reinforcements, though so far they were holding their own. Thereupon 'A' Squadron was despatched to his assistance, while the Police Squadron and 'C' Squadron of the M.R.F., under Capt. Drury, and Major Kershaw respectively, galloped across some mealie fields to the foot of Sikombo's hill where they left their horses under cover and proceeded to storm the position on foot. The ascent was most difficult, was rendered the more unpleasant by a terrific fire from the enemy, who found shelter in innumerable caves and behind great boulders of granite. The sides of the hill were almost vertical, and it was only with the utmost care that a foothold could be obtained at all. The summit, however, was almost reached when Major Kershaw, well to the front, was shot through the body and fell mortally wounded. Sgt.-Major McCloskie, of 'C' Squadron, who was close on his heels, fell almost at the same instant.

On the summit of an adjacent kopje which was secured by Capt. Beresford, a portion of the Police Squadron, acting in co-operation with 'D' Squadron and the Maxim of the M.R.F. put to flight a large number of rebels with heavy slaughter. They had first however, to encounter a terrible fusillade, and at one time a concerted charge of the Matabele, in which Sgt.-Major Ainslie, of the M.M.P. fell shot through the head. On a slight hill to the left, the M.M.P. Maxim, under Capt. Hoel Llewellyn, was doing great things, the officer in command displaying the greatest heroism. Endeavouring not to needlessly expose his men he ordered them to take cover while he manipulated the gun single handed, and swept down the rebels as they rushed in large numbers to carry the place. But a gallant young trooper, Evelyn Holmes, who was orderly to the adjutant, deeming that the odds against his officer were too heavy rushed to his assistance and paid for his bravery with his life, being shot the moment he gained the gun.

By this time British reinforcements were seen advancing through the valley, and the insurgents confined themselves to defensive works, lining the sides and tops to the hills adjacent to Sikombo's whence they were only driven after a stubborn resistance. Between two and three o'clock the 'Assembly' was sounded, and the Column moved off towards their base. The return march was necessarily slow, owing to the number of wounded, thirteen in all.

One officer and four sergeant-majors were killed in the action, and two of the wounded, an officer and a trooper died shortly afterwards. The former of the two, Lieut. Hervey, said as he lay waiting for his approaching end, 'Well, I suppose before long I shall be extending the British Empire on Jupiter or somewhere else.' Only a few weeks before he had been appointed Civil Commissioner for Barotseland.

In the 'Orders' read out at general parade on Sunday, Aug. 8th, it was announced that the Column was to march off into the hills once more that night. The march would be conducted in strict silence, no smoking or 'dop' would be allowed, and the objective would be the stronghold of Umlugulu, the paramount chief of a large tract of the hill country. The troops moved away at midnight, under a clear and starlit sky. The hills soon closed around them and their progress became most difficult, the whole column being obliged to come to a dead stop every few yards, owing to the nature of the ground. One mounted troop became hopelessly 'bushed,' and after wandering aimlessly among the rocks for some hours, returned to camp, taking with them the food supply and the blankets of the Scouts and others in front, who later on had much to say of their desertion. Shortly afterwards, two or three other important sections of the column went astray, and had anyone been attacked by the insurgents a terrible disaster would inevitably have occurred. As a matter of fact, the Ambulance Corps, together with about a hundred friendlies, did wander into the heart of an invisible impi. As Babayana himself stated later, 'You were so close to us that we could have rolled rocks down and killed everyone of you.' The main column had emerged from the valley, however, and scaled the heights, ridge by ridge, until at last the summit of the main range was gained. Here a magnificent panorama of the Matopos met the eye of the troops, extending for miles and miles of glittering bald peaks and valleys, frowning gorges, broken kopjes, and bush clad slopes, the whole converted to a lovely work of light and shade by the rays of the sun. Immediately below, to the left, lay a bird's eye view of the field of the last engagement.

At eight o'clock, the mountain battery brought to bear on some kraals which, after a bombardment, proved to be deserted. Two hours later the column took up a position on a bare plateau which commanded an extensive view of the hills occupied by the enemy, and the valley that lay between. The Police guns immediately began to shell the heights with ring and shrapnel. The gunners were by this time practised, and kept up their work at a range of 1,200 yards with great speed and precision, the fire lasting for well over an hour. During the afternoon, some cattle were captured and driven into a rock kraal near the British position, then the column settled down for the night.

Just before sundown, rifle fire was opened from the right front by the rebels, who had advanced unseen under cover of the rocks. They were welcomed by the guns, as well as rifles, and retired, their retreat being followed up by the Cape Boys. That night again was spent on the hill top, a bitterly cold wind was blowing and, towards midnight, there was a rain storm; and as most of the men had no blankets or greatcoats, there was not much sleep in store for them. The rebels, however, made no further attempt on the position and, at dawn, the Column started on the return journey to camp. It was learnt afterwards that the enemy had hoped to draw the Column further into the hills where they were so disposed as to intercept progress and cause a repetition of the scene at 'Laing's Graveyard.' But as it happened, the last shot of the Matabele Rebellion had been fired and shortly afterwards, through the pluck and diplomacy of Cecil Rhodes, peace was declared, and the men of the relief column were enabled to proceed to their home.

CHAPTER TWENTY FOUR

The Modern B.S.A.P. – The Rising in Mashonaland
– Wholesale Massacre – Capt. Nesbitt wins the V.C.
– The Concentrated Essence of Several Miracles

As a result of the Jameson Raid, the control of the Chartered Co.'s Police forces was taken from the hands of the Rhodesian authorities by the Imperial Government. On October 18th 1896, while the war was still waging in Matabeleland, the Mashonaland Mounted Police, the Matabeleland Mounted Police, together with what remained of the old B.B.P. were amalgamated, the resultant corps being known by its present name, 'The British South Africa Police.' The Commandant-General, who was also Deputy Commissioner, acted as the representative of the High Commissioner. In Rhodesia the authorised strength was as follows: Mashonaland, 500; Matabeleland, 600; Native contingent, 300. Supreme command was allotted to Colonel Richard Martin, K.C.M.G., an Imperial officer. The Commandant of the Mashonaland Division was the Hon. Frederick Rossmore Eveleigh de Moleyns, D.S.O., who was assisted by Chief Inspector Audley Vaughan Gosling. In Matabeleland the Commandant was Col. John Sanctuary Nicholson, while William Bodle acted as Chief Inspector. Col. Walford had charge of the Bechuanaland Division, whose headquarters were at Mafeking.

The newly formed regiment was to be blooded at its birth. Three months after the outbreak in Matabeleland the Mashonas rose in revolt and indulged in wholesale massacres even more horrible than those that had been wrought in the sister province. No one had dreamed that the hitherto peaceful Mashona were capable of the atrocities committed by their conquerors. For years they lived as slaves, until the coming of the White man had freed them and enabled them to live at peace with all men. They had been known as timid hard working agriculturists, content to work for the strong race that had befriended them, knowing that they would be rewarded for their services in full, and be shielded as well from any depredations such as they had they had been accustomed to endure in the past. It was even thought that they had a real sense of the virtue of gratitude, a virtue that was totally nonexistent among the savage Matabele or their Zulu forefathers. The result of this misplaced confidence on the part of the settlers was that the best of the manhood of Mashonaland had been drained away by the call of the rebellion in Matabeleland. There was but a handful of the old Mashonaland Mounted Police, while the civilians – a great number of them members of the old Police and Pioneer columns – had sallied forth from their various districts to take part in the final crushing of the menace that threatened Bulawayo and the country round. So it was that the news of this new trouble came upon the little crowd of settlers like a thunderbolt.

The Mashona had been carefully primed by envoys of the Matabele with the news of the wholesale massacres that their impis had been engaged upon, and these stories, of course, were exaggerated until it seemed to the more simple natives in the East as though the valour of the white man was utterly useless when pitted against the skill and shrewdness of the Matabele. Loot on a large scale was promised to all those who could pluck up sufficient spirit to participate in a general rising. The Matabele could not fail to win, for their part, and if the Mashona would but join in the victory, they would be treated as the equals of their former tyrants. The old days were past, and they would never again be molested in any way. The Eastern natives listened to all this with a ready ear. Work in the mines and in the fields was not the tasteful thing that their new White lords had pictured it to them. These same lords had brought the locust into the country, a thing that had never been known before their advent, which was devastating the native crops and threatening the people with starvation.

Such was the origin of the rising in Mashonaland. The first massacres, which were instigated by small bands of Matabele, took place at Hartley and Mazoe. The news of the rebellion spread like wildfire and in three days almost the entire Mashona nation had taken to their guns and assegais. More than one hundred white men, women and children, fell within the first few days of the rising, together with several hundred unarmed and friendly natives whose crime was that they were working for their white masters. The people of Salisbury rushed to safety into laager at the gaol, which had previously been

119

fortified. Similar laagers were formed at Victoria, Charter, Enkeldoorn, Melsetter and Umtali. Horses and ammunition were most scarce so that the work of the rescue parties were greatly hindered, but volunteer corps were quickly formed, every able bodied man in the community entering into military service.

The Rhodesia Horse recruited in Mashonaland for work in the former rebellion, hurried back as fast as their horses could carry them from Matabeleland, arriving in Salisbury simultaneously with a Bulawayo relief patrol under Capt. White. At the same time a force of Imperial regulars – hussars and mounted infantry under Lieut.-Col Alderson were making their way from Cape Town by the way of Beira. The little army, regulars, volunteers and police were at once engaged in hard fighting that proved even more strenuous than the warfare in Matabeleland. Patrols scoured the country in all directions. There were few pitched battles, as the Mashona never once stood in the open, but ran like baboons to the shelter of the hills and there they had fortresses more impregnable than any in the Matopos, places where none but a native could swarm up the almost perpendicular smooth granite to the summits of the hills where their grain and their cattle lay concealed. The lack of horses proved the greatest handicap to the work of rescue, and the lives of those of the outside settlers who had not been murdered lay in the greatest suspense, huddled together in little groups not knowing what day was to be their last. It was not until many weeks after the outbreak that the parties beleaguered at the Abercorn goldfields and the Hartley Hills were relieved. The heavy toll of the men killed in action spoke for the efforts of the rescuers, but meanwhile the heavy slaughter among the almost defenceless miners and farmers grew even larger.

Heavy fighting took place at the start in the near vicinity of Salisbury. Mr. Justice Vincent, who was placed at the head of affairs in the town, speedily organised a defence committee and succeeded in raising a force of 350 men, with 60 Police. About 250 guns were collected and issued to them. One of the earliest events was the gallant rescue of a party of twelve who gathered at the Alice Mine in the Mazoe district 27 miles from the capital. On this occasion the Police secured the highest military honour the world has to offer – the coveted V.C. which was gained by Captain (now Major) R. Nesbitt, on June 20th 1896. Two of the beleaguered party, which included three women, had heroically volunteered to cut their way through the enemy to the telegraph office, where they could call for help. They were successful in sending their message, but were killed in trying to regain the laager. On receipt of the telegram, Mr Judson, Director of Telegraphs, galloped out from Salisbury with five men, but found the situation at the laager so desperate that he sent a message back to the capital asking for a force of at least 100 men and a Maxim, as the whole Mazoe Valley was lined with natives some 1,000 strong. Capt. Nesbitt, who had already set out with 12 men to reinforce Mr. Judson's patrol, intercepted the note at the head of the valley. The officer asked his little force if they were content to join him in attempting a rescue. They unanimously decided to do so, and pushed on through the danger zone. With the utmost courage and temerity they succeeded in gaining the shelter of the laager. Placing the women in an armour plated wagon, they started to cut their way back again, travelling under heavy fire the whole time. A rear-guard and an advance-guard were hastily formed. Soon after quitting the road that branched off to the Alice, a shot or two greeted their approach. The advance-guard were wasting ammunition by at-random shooting into the long grass, and word was sent forward telling them to be more careful. The enemy's fire became brisker as they proceeded. The natives were quite invisible and the only aim that could be taken was directed at the puffs of smoke that issued from the trees and grass on the hills and by the river. The little party were still showing a tendency to shoot wildly. Suddenly one man, McGeer, was seen to fall, and his body had to be left where it lay. Shots from the Mashona were now coming thick and fast, and many of the party were hit slightly. The rebels were on all sides, and they were being continually reinforced. Several of the horses were killed and sometimes the rear-guard was forced right back to the wagon. The hard work was gradually tiring out those who had no mounts, and they had frequently to hold on to the wagon or jump on to the steps where they could recover their breath.

After going seven miles, they reached a place where a steep hillside ran down to the road. It was thronged with excited savages, who overflowed into the long grass at the opposite side of the road. The natives behind, many of them mounted, pressed on more vigorously than before. Firing was now point blank and the wheeler mules were killed. These were replaced by horses, but those animals again were killed immediately. At last the party had to discard wheelers altogether. Two more men were killed, one of the advance-guard was wounded in the face, and another, who had been at the side of the wagon looking after the women, was shot clean through the head, the bullet entering under the ear and making it's exit at the cheek bone opposite. Curiously enough he never even fell, but crawled along and entered the wagon. One gallant horse which had been hit in the head carried its rider for miles. Two of the mounted men now dashed through to the town in search for help, but none could be spared, and the party had to continue to do the best it could.

More ambuscades were passed, and several bullets went through the top of the wagon, the iron sheets being dotted in scores of places with bullets and slugs. There was a tank underneath the cart, but it could not be got at without a halt, and so the wounded men were obliged to go without water.

The whole party were enduring the utmost exhaustion, and their sufferings were terrible. However, at last their difficulties were overcome and they managed to arrive in Salisbury with the loss of three men killed and five wounded. As one of the survivors said at the time, 'It was the concentrated essence of several miracles that any of us came out of it alive.'

Col. Alderson's force of 380 regulars reached Salisbury on August 9th, having relieved Umtali en route. Alderson remained five months in the country and although greatly hampered by the shortage of supplies, he effected the capture of an important chief, Makoni, and the destruction of numerous rebel kraals, finally attacking and taking the stronghold of the powerful Matshayangombi, the real leader of the rebellion, It was now considered – wrongly, as was afterwards seen – that the trouble had been concluded, and that the settlement of the country might safely be left to Sir Richard Martin, who had at the time a Police force of 580 Whites and 100 N.P. The Imperial troops left Rhodesia on November 29th 1896.

CHAPTER TWENTY FIVE

A Great Task for the Police – The Rebels Hold Out – The Death of Matshayangombi – A Tough Nigger – Peace once More

It now fell to the B.S.A.P. to carry through an achievement which should always be regarded as one of the most brilliant they have ever performed. It was their work to succeed where the Imperial army had failed, and if they had not shown perseverance, endurance, gallantry, and discipline of the highest in their execution of the task, success could never have been theirs. On the departure of Alderson it was thought that nothing remained to be done but to police the country, in the most limited sense of the word, and to prevent a few unruly natives from reaping the crops that were then being sown. In November, it was reported that all the chiefs were desirous of peace and that there was not the slightest fear of any further acts of rebellion. But the withdrawal of the force that had defeated Matshayangombi at Hartley had left that powerful chief in possession of several minor strongholds that had not been destroyed. These were strengthened and reoccupied, hosts of refugee Matabele Native Police and other rebels flocked to join the insurgents, the two leading priests of the 'M'limo' arrived to use their influence on the side of prolonged resistance, and the rebels became more confident than ever. The chiefs in the neighbourhood of the capital secretly resolved, while outwardly professing peace, to make every effort to drive the whites out of the country.

In December, the settlement of the country was entrusted to the Police, the force then consisting of 580 whites and a 100 native contingent. Col. De Moleyns at once began to organise a fighting force of 250 police and 400 volunteers, with 120 natives. The Native Police recruited at the time, 90 of them from Zululand, formed a magnificent body of warriors who did most invaluable work throughout the campaign. One hundred and eighty of the white recruits had hastened up in search of active service from Cape Town and Natal. During the month, Hartley

Hill was occupied by 'B' Troop of the Police, under Major Hopper. In January, a further detachment left with Col. de Moleyns and formed a post, Fort Mandora, close to the kraal of Matshayangombi. It was seen, however, that the native position was too strong to be attacked by the force then available. Col. de Moleyns' post was withdrawn and another fort erected within 900 yards of the stronghold, containing a 7-pounder and a Maxim, with about 20 men and a few natives. All they could do until July was to keep lookout on the stronghold, harass its occupants in a small way, and destroy the crops that grew in the open vleis. Occasionally a man was wounded but the little force soon found that their greatest sufferings were to result from the lack of wholesome food. Fortunately, they had a good supply of quinine with which to contend against the daily attacks of fever. Desultory fighting continued without cessation until the final engagement. On one occasion, the rebels made a determined attack on the post, but were repulsed after severe fighting. All this time frequent attempts were made to induce the rebels to surrender, and on one occasion Matshayangombi sent in a few guns and some money, stating that he wished for peace, but, on the demand being made for the surrender of a reasonable number of guns, made no response and resumed his attitude of defiance. Meanwhile many posts were established at points commanding the kopjes held by the principal chiefs, and harassing tactics were systematically adopted until the cessation of the rains, when the Commandant-General was able to take more active steps. At the end of the year Major Gosling dispersed bands of rebels who had been raiding in the Charter district, and in January Sekki's kopje was taken, with a considerable amount of loot. In February the strongholds of two powerful chiefs, Chiquaqua and Soswe were captured by a combined force of volunteers and police from Umtali. Simultaneously a flying patrol made an assault on Matshayangombi's kraal, but was repulsed.

In March, the Police in the fighting columns were considerably augmented, and by April when most of the volunteers had been discharged, their strength had grown to 566. During the first month they cleared the central portion of the Mazoe district, putting the most important chief to flight, and visited Matokos, where they persuaded an important contingent of friendlies to march with them.

In April the Mangwendi rebels received the severest blow that the insurgents had yet felt and a fight at Shaungwe marked the commencement of the series of decisive attacks which finally crushed the rebellion. Kunzwi and Mashanganyika, the two leading allies of Matshayangombi, were attacked with the most complete success and a large number of Police were now left available for the more strenuous work in the Hartley District. They were reinforced by 200 Imperial Hussars, who with 50 Matabele Police and 40 Cape Boys, had arrived in Mashonaland from Bulawayo. The combined column was divided into two, each taking a different route to the point in the Hartley district where they had arranged to meet. En route several kraals were destroyed and marauding parties dealt with by one column while the other successfully negotiated a pitched battle on the Hunyani river, taking some strongly held kopjes and a large number of prisoners.

At Hartley the total force available for the assault on the stronghold of the paramount chief amounted to 460 whites, and 210 natives, with machine guns and a 12½.-pounder. The attack was delivered on July 24th. The column charged in three parties, and the battle became a repetition of most of those that had already taken place in Mashonaland, a slow but sure climb up an impregnable position, in the face of a terrible hail of assegais and rifle fire. As in the other engagements the extraordinary confidence and gallantry of the Britishers gained the day. The rebels, after a stubborn resistance were driven from the stronghold. As they were retreating, a Police trooper named Blyth, who had left his work in the regimental armoury to volunteer for the more congenial labour of a fighting man, noticed a prominent figure running at the head of the rebels, although hampered by a heavy greatcoat which had apparently been donned as a badge of rank. Raising his rifle the trooper took steady aim and fired, thus practically putting an end to the campaign, for the native he had killed proved to be Matshayangombi, the unusually daring Mashona chieftain who had been the leader and guiding light of the rebellion. The caves and stone fortifications were completely destroyed with dynamite, and an incident occurred which well illustrated the wonderful toughness and endurance of the African warrior. A Mashona had taken refuge in one of the caves prior to its destruction. The sounds of the explosion were still echoing among the neighbouring hills when he was seen to emerge from the mouth of the cavern. Both his legs had been blown away at the knee, but he came out at a run and it was not until he had descended to the very base of the great kopje that he finally fell.

The Police were now divided into several columns which swept the country in parallel lines between Hartley and the main road. The next concerted move was towards Lomagundi. The Police established a post at Sinoia, and a small detachment of Hussars patrolled the southern part of the district. But all resistance was over. The chiefs and people surrendered freely; 2,000 guns, including a limited number of breechloaders, had been given up, and at the close of September it was announced that the rebellion was at an end, and the services of the Hussars could be dispensed with.

The B.S.A.P. turned to the ordinary work of a Colonial police force, preventing and detecting crime, making tracks through the wilderness, surveying, erecting telegraph and telephone systems and in general doing the groundwork that has to-day made Rhodesia one of the most promising and most rapidly developing young countries that this or any other empire has ever known, whose greatest boast should be that in twenty-four years it has become a land which can be traversed by a stranger from end to end, without a weapon of any sort. The system of small out-stations that still survives was now systematically adopted, with larger headquarter stations in each of the rising townships. In Mashonaland new kraals were located in open ground. The rising had shown that kraals situated in the almost inaccessible rock kopjes would always provide a menace, making it the easiest thing in the world for natives to elude forces sent against them, by simply retiring from one kopje to another.

CHAPTER TWENTY SIX

Plumer's Task – Skirmishing on the Crocodile River
– The Gallant Fight at Bryce's Store
– The Boers retire from the Territory
– Captain Llewellyn and the Armoured Trains

At the outbreak of the Boer War in Oct. 1899, the total strength of the three divisions of Police amounted to 1,106. Two months before, Col. Baden-Powell, the shrewd fighter and scout of Matopos fame, had arrived in Bulawayo to organise a Frontier Defence Force whose headquarters would be on the railway line at Mafeking, but whose operations would extend along the Limpopo to Tuli and embrace the whole frontier of Bechuanaland and Rhodesia adjoining the Transvaal. His second in command was Col. Plumer, who had also done brilliant work in the previous campaign. For Mafeking and the district, the strength of the Protectorate Regiment was increased and requisitions were made from the B.S.A.P. After the investment of the town, the command of the Northern wing devolved entirely on Plumer who had by then established his base at Tuli.

From the commencement of hostilities things looked as black as they could well have been. A distinct fear was felt that the Boers might make an attack in force on the territory, and the 500 miles from Mafeking to the north-eastern point of Transvaal formed a tremendous frontier to guard effectively, in the event of invasion. It was further to be expected that the natives, only finally quieted by parley after the terrible bloodshed of '96, would once again rebel. In July, the hut tax had resulted in an exhibition of threatening language from a hitherto loyal kraal in the Victoria district. The loyalty of the four Great Bechuana chiefs could not absolutely be relied upon. The Rhodesian troops were completely cut off from the Cape ports on which they naturally depended, and the only line of communication from Tuli lay through Rhodesia as follows:- to Bulawayo, 200 miles, and thence to Salisbury, 280 miles of ox transport, thence to the Portuguese port of Beira, 380 miles of rail. A further difficulty, one which made the hopelessness of the situation appear to be almost insurmountable lay in the fact that it was not for many months that the Portuguese Government decided to allow munitions of war to pass over Beira line. The last and only orders received by Plumer from his superior before the relief of Mafeking were:- '(1) To defend the border as far as it could be carried out from the neighbourhood of Tuli as a centre; (2) By a display of strength to induce the Boers to detail a strong force to protect their northern district; (3) To create a diversion in the north of the Transvaal, cooperating with the invasion of the south by our main force, if necessary advancing into the Transvaal for the purpose. No portion of your forces is to cross the frontier till you receive orders; instructions will be sent to you as to the date for cooperation with the other column.' It was seven months before Plumer had any tidings of a southern column, and he had to trust to his own initiative on the imprisonment of his superior in the beleaguered town, acting for the best on his own responsibility.

Fort Tuli, constructed during the progress of the Pioneer March that led to the occupation of Mashonaland, lay some 40 miles north of Rhodes Drift on the Crocodile River. A large tributary ran by the place, supplying it with good water, while the position, consisting of earth-works erected about two neighbouring kopjes, was a strong one. Plumer entered the fort on Oct. 16th with 420 of the Rhodesian Regiment, a force chiefly recruited at Port Elizabeth, with one Rhodesian squadron, 80 B.S.A.P., and a battery consisting of a 12½ -pounder, one 2.5in. gun and two Maxims, under Captain Hoel Llewellyn of the B.S.A.P. The remainder of the troops in the territory consisted of about 520 B.S.A.P. in Matabeleland, and the Southern Rhodesia Volunteers, about 1,050 strong, and 380 B.S.A.P. in Mashonaland. There were a further two 2.5in. guns, two 7-pounders, and six Gatlings and Maxims. Altogether, there were no more than 2,500 to defend the territory more than twice as large as England and Wales, and to assist in some way in the relief of Mafeking. It must be stated that the ever ready settlers had done all they could. Before the conclusion of the war they sent 1,500 men to the front, a percentage of 12½ of their whole white population; a force far larger in proportion to that despatched from any other portion of the Empire.

At the various drifts along the Crocodile, Col. Bodle had

already established patrols about 100 strong of the Police. From Oct. 19th, when a reconnoitring patrol first sighted the Boers, there was almost daily skirmishing. On the 26th, 6 Boers were killed, and 4 captured. The bushy country which contained large stretches of romantic palm forest, offered equal opportunities to either side, whose methods of fighting were again most similar as a result of the natural training of the men engaged, and for some time the honours may be said to have been even. On Nov. 2nd, however, the burgers invaded the colony in force, crossing at Bryce's Store and Rhodes' Drift. 16 of the Police with two young lieutenants, Hare and Haserick were at the former place, whither they convoyed six wagons from Tuli. The store was a sturdy building of brick, capable of being defended for a long time against rifle fire. Early in the morning of the 2nd, the escort were seated at breakfast, two troopers being despatched toward the river to guard against alarm. The morning meal was still in progress when the party were startled by the return of the couple who were galloping furiously, their horses and equipment torn by the cruel thorns they had encountered in their ride. They reported the approach of a large body of horse.

The wagons were hastily formed into a laager and a messenger was at once sent to the telephone line to communicate with Tuli, but it was found that the line was cut, together with the wire leading to Rhodes' Drift, which was held by the Rhodesian Regiment, under Col. Spreckley. The Boers emerged from the shelter of the bush some two hundred yards away from the wagons. The garrison greeted them with a brisk volley and they were soon driven back to shelter. Firing went on for some time, but the burghers could make no effect on the staunch little band of defenders, who were taking keen aim from the windows of the building as well as from the shade of the wagons. Suddenly, however, big guns were brought into action from the rear. The range was soon found and the shells fell thick and fast. One came through the roof of the store, another entered a window, and it was obvious that in another quarter of an hour the whole structure would be smashed to pieces. Still there was no word of surrender, neither the thin walls or the low wagons gave any sort of protection from shell fire, and it was decided to make a dash for the bush. In the rush several were wounded, amongst them being the Rev. J. Leary, a chaplain who had accompanied the convoy. These men, seven in all, were captured. The rest of the party got safely back to camp. It was learned afterwards that the burgher force which the handful had striven against so valiantly consisted of no less than 1,500 fighting men with a Hotchkiss and seven-pounder-guns.

During the whole of November the tiny legions held the enemy at bay, forcing them to imagine that they were opposed by over 1,400 instead of the paltry 500 that were actually in the field. The fight at Bryce's store and a simultaneous reverse by the Rhodesia Regiment at Rhodes' Drift had forced Plumer to move back on Tuli, leaving the Boers for three weeks in possession of the drifts, but the invaders were never allowed time to feel secure. No breathing space was given them. They were harassed day and night, their pickets were surprised and sniped. Their outposts were raided. Small skirmishes between detached patrols were incessant, and the game became not at all monotonous to the sporting Rhodesian, who soon proved to be far more watchful, irritating and troublesome than their wily enemy. The burgers at last had met with opponents who, to their astonishment and disgust, beat them at their own game. The commandoes became discontented, and, after a short time, practically abandoned aggressive tactics. They began to dribble back towards the south, the departure of the various units being accelerated by the always disquieting attentions of Plumer's men.

At last the territory was rid of them altogether. On Nov. 2nd, Plumer made a thorough reconnaissance along the river for 200 miles. On Dec. 1st he led a flying column of almost his full strength into the Transvaal, to within 50 miles of Pietersburg without meeting a single scout from the enemy. On the 19th he again went as far as Wegdraai, on the Brak River. The Boers had evidently abandoned the frontier along the Crocodile, but patrolling was kept up, occasional glimpses being secured of hostile parties who, however, were little more than marauding bands, with no desire for fighting. This task was extremely arduous for the small patrols, who would infinitely have preferred some show of real scrapping, with the glory that was to be won therein.

On Boxing Day, sports were held by the B.S.A.P. and the Rhodesian Regiment, and on the following day the C.O., leaving 120 men and a 12½-pounder at Tuli and 20 at Macloutsie, left for Palapye with 400 men, a 2.5in. gun and a Maxim. He was now free to proceed more directly towards the clearance of the

Western border south of Mafeking.

During Plumer's absence at Tuli, the operations down the line towards the beleaguered town had been directed by Col. Nicholson, of the Police, from Bulawayo. It was known on the second day of the campaign (Oct. 12th 1899) that communication with the south was cut off, and instant steps were taken to prevent the destruction of the railway line. A search train was despatched southwards, while the artificers in the railway workshops at Bulawayo began the construction of armoured trains capable of withstanding rifle shots and penetrating the districts occupied by the Boers. Four of these were completed and despatched by the 19th Oct., manned by detachments of the B.S.A.P, and the Southern Rhodesia Volunteers. Meanwhile large commandoes had been located at Lobatsi, at Deerdepoort near Mochudi, and at Selika Kop on the Crocodile.

The first armoured train arrived at Crocodile Pools on Oct. 16th with Capt. Llewellyn and 200 men, Police and railway employees. On the following day a cautious advance was made to within three miles of Lobatsi, where the line was found to be torn up. The Boers were reported to be advancing north and it was decided to await them. On the 18th, the first engagement occurred. It was learned from the scouts that a strong body of Boers had congregated on kopjes and in a spruit about a mile and a half south of Crocodile Pools bent on the further destruction of the line and an attack on the train. The armoured engine was placed between an armoured and sandbagged truck, holding forty men, and slowly steamed along the line. The Maxim gave tongue to locate the enemy, and at once secured a reply. Volleys of rifle fire were directed towards the kopje, whence the Boers were driven to the shelter of the river bed. Many of them fell in the retreat. The train proceeded steadily, Capt. Llewellyn swaying the Maxim wherever a movement was visible. Only ten shots in all hit the trucks and the British suffered no casualties. The Boer Commandant was injured by a throw from his horse, which was shot.

A second advance was made on the 21st. The second armoured train had now arrived as a reinforcement and a more formidable passage of arms ensued. Late in the afternoon some 250 mounted Boers, with wagons and mules, were located in open ground nearly two thousand yards from the line, where they evidently thought themselves to be out of reach of their opponents. Capt. Llewellyn steamed abreast of the party, found their range with a single shot from the Maxim and began to mow them down like so much hay. The rest of the engagement was short and sweet. The survivors scattered in a panic, and fled, with a loss of sixty killed and wounded and a great number of horses and mules. Two days later the Boers were found hard at work building fortifications capable of mounting big guns, and on the 24th it was heard that a commando of 500, with three guns, had reinforced the earlier body. The Rhodesians promptly decided to remove all material that night to the siding at Gaberones, as the trains could not face shells. Mahalapye, where there was a good water supply, was selected as the base of operations, and Mochudi as the southern point to be held. The native chief Linchwe had his young men armed and patrolling the country, and they acted as most efficient scouts, detailing every movement of the enemy. Nothing more was to be done for the present but to keep the trains patrolling up and down the line, and to make observations from such altitudes as Basuto Kopje, near Crocodile Pools.

A further detachment of B.S.A.P. and S.R.V. left Bulawayo for the front on Oct. 22nd. At Mahalapye forts were erected and a strong camp formed, and by Nov. 3rd, the fifth and sixth armoured trains were despatched. Three weeks later, many strong preparations were made for an advance in force.

CHAPTER TWENTY SEVEN

Deerdepoort – An Artillery Duel
– Major Bird's Failure – Von Dalwig Tribute
– Nearing Ramathlabama – Mafeking

The enemy suffered a severe blow on Nov. 25th. They had established a laager at Deerdepoort in the Transvaal, and the commandoes had been raiding Linchwe's cattle from the Kaffir 'Stad', Sequani, over the border. On the night of the 24th, Col. Holdsworth, of the S.R.V., with a force of 108 Police and Volunteers, set out to reconnoitre the position and note the strength of the laager. The Rhodesians were advanced to within about five hundred yards of the Boer position, Capt. Llewellyn with a Police Maxim in the centre, Capt. Drury with the B.S.A.P. on the right and the S.R.V. on the left. Firing commenced at daybreak and the line slowly advanced. But the seven hundred of Linchwe's warriors had followed close on the heels of the burghers and, seeing the successful commencement of the attack, they left the drift where they lay in hiding and made a sudden advance on their own, firing at the Boers as they came. This unexpected assistance was totally undesirable to the British commander, who withdrew his men and returned to camp. Of the 80 Boers who had occupied the laager, between 50 and 60 were killed or wounded in the engagement.

During December and January the troops were engaged making good their advance and reconnoitring the railway line. Plumer was no longer occupied by the defence of the Crocodile border, and was able to turn his attention to the Boer artillery that commanded the railway. The enemy's position lay on a range of hills running obliquely to, and finally crossing the line south of Crocodile Pools Station. Near the centre of their position, on the summit of the highest kopje, they had built an open stone fort, wherein was mounted a 12½-pounder Vickers-Maxim quick firer. On adjoining ridges were also a 5-pounder and a pom-pom. These guns were manned by experts of the Staats Artillerie, under the command of a German officer, Capt. von Dalwig. The whole Boer force was commanded by Sarel

Eloff, a grandson of President Kruger. One night the Rhodesians were cheered by the news that a train had rolled in from Bulawayo with a 12½-pounder to reinforce their two obsolete 7-pounders. The 12½- pounder was hurried down to the Metsimaklaba Bridge to give some sort of answer to the enemy's big gun which, as usual, opened fire during the forenoon. For three hours there was brisk cannonading, Father Hartmann, S.J., the Police chaplain, who recorded every shot fired, putting the number down at one hundred and seventy-two. But the Rhodesian gun was without epaulement or protection of any kind, and stood right in the open, while the excellent artillery work of the Staats Artillerie, at a range of 5,000 yards, made things so hot that it was considered advisable to withdraw out of range.

It was decided that our gunners would have a better chance with a masked shell-proof battery at a very much closer range. A position was chosen in the rocky bed of the Notwani River, hidden by a luxuriant growth of timber. It was only after a liberal use of the axe that the outline of the Boer fort could be brought without obstruction in line with the gun sights. The railway engineers worked with a will, and in two or three days a substantial battery was completed, built of steel rails, sleepers and sand-bags, and flanked by heavy earth-works. The fort was disguised by a screen of bushes, quite indistinguishable at a short distance from the neighbouring woodland.

The railwaymen now set to work to raise the Metsimaklaba Bridge, dynamited by the Boers, but were greatly hindered in their task by shellfire, always directed with the greatest judgment and accuracy. To cover their operations, Plumer occupied three kopjes east and west of the bridge, his position being nearly parallel to that of the Boers. The hills were known as Maclaren's Kopje, Basuto Kopje, and Fortress Kopje. Between them and the Boer position lay an extensive plateau covered with thick bush, broken here and there by an open glade. Basuto Kopje a small but commanding position 200 yards from the bridge, was a precipitous rock, 150 feet high, difficult of ascent and affording good cover. It was surmounted by a Maxim. At the foot of the hill the Metsimaklaba flowed eastward, uniting with the Notwani a few hundred yards lower down. Fortress Kopje, a long isolated hill, rose abruptly from the level plain half a mile to the east. Its sides and summit were covered with stone breastworks probably constructed by

Msilikatse during the northern advent of his Zulu impis. These walls were improved by Plumer's men into most formidable loop-holed schanzes capable of giving the warmest of warm receptions to Brother Boer, should he take it into his head to pay a surprise visit.

There were only 100 men available to guard the widely separated line of posts. However, it was always possible even on a bright day to note the moment of the discharge of the enemy's big gun, and their constant cannonade was barren, not a man on the British side being killed by their gunnery, extraordinary accurate as it was.

At last, with the aid of a couple of 20-ton jacks and wedges, the bridge was raised to the level of the permanent way. At the same time a shell proof battery was erected for the two 7-pounders which, however, proved of little use except to divert the enemy's attention from the working parties, as their range was deficient and they fired black powder; betraying their whereabouts at every shot. The completion of the bridge strengthened Plumer's hand considerably, as he could now secure the co-operation of the armoured trains in any offensive advance movement.

Early in February, two successive night attacks were planned for the capture of the Boer fort. Nearly 500 men were detailed for the work and, as there were many miles to be traversed, the force mustered at sunset at the base camp and began their march over the thorn clad plain. No superfluous equipment was carried and the men paraded in their 'greyback' shirts, the sleeves rolled up above the elbow. There was no moon and progress was slow, but the troopers were filled with enthusiasm at the prospect of a scrap at last. Suddenly there was a crash of thunder, a vivid flash of lightning and the rain began to fall as it can only fall in Africa. The veldt lay under a vast sheet of water. It was hopeless to proceed and the order was given to return. Disappointed and soaked to the skin, the column made its way back. The attack was postponed till the following night, but there was a further storm, even more violent than the last, and once more the idea of taking the fort by assault was temporarily abandoned.

On Feb. 12th, however, in the early morn, Major Bird, of the Rhodesian Regiment, negotiated the ascent of the Boer Kopje with a following of 200 men, Police, S.R.V. and the Rhodesian Regiment. Half way up the hill their approach was discovered and they were greeted by a heavy rifle fire, which was reinforced by case from the 12½-pounder as they neared the summit. A mine was exploded beneath them and their advance was obstructed by barbed-wire entanglements, huge boulders and abattis of felled trees. The Rhodesians had received orders on no account to fire a shot but to trust to their cold steel at the top, and doggedly continued on their way in silence with set teeth in spite of all the obstacles.

For a few yards from the fort to the crest of the kopje there was natural stone glacis and as the assaulting party endeavoured to get at close quarters with their opponents they were exposed to a veritable hail of bullets. Men began to fall on all sides. Capt. French, in the van, was killed at the entrance to the fort, Major Straker, of the Police, fell shot through the breast. It was dark and the men did not know the ground. Hence not more than about half of them found their way to the top of the hill. In a few minutes, thirty of the Rhodesians were killed and wounded without firing a shot. Then slowly and reluctantly, the attackers fell back carrying most of their wounded with them. So at break of dawn, their comrades at the base camp saw them emerge from the bush straggling along with torn clothing and bleeding hands and faces, with a fixed resolve to retrieve the present disaster at a later date. The daring attack had at least instilled a genuine respect for Plumer's men in the hearts of the burgher soldiers. Capt. von Dalwig, the German artilleryman, showed a manly appreciation of British bravery by erecting a large stone cairn, surmounted by a wooden cross bearing the inscription:-

'Here Capt. French fell. He was a brave man. If any of his relatives would like to know any details of his death I shall be glad to give them when the war is over, if I am spared. Signed; P von Dalwig, Staats Art.'

It was learnt afterwards that he had shot the young officer with his own hand while he endeavoured to cut the barbed wire at the entrance to the fort.

On the 16th, the Boers, reinforced from Mafeking, attempted to follow up their victory with a counterstroke, but were repulsed by a patrol under Lieut. Blunt. Shortly afterwards they evacuated Crocodile Pools, to take part in the assault on Mafeking. On the following day Major Bird captured a Boer laager near Gopani, ten miles to the east. Plumer now discovered that the enemy, greatly discouraged by tidings of the relief of Kimberley and Ladysmith, and the surrender of Cronje at Paardeberg, had resolved at least to effect the capture of Mafeking, and had summoned practically all the commandoes within reach for that purpose. He determined to push forward reconnoitring forces, in the hope of withdrawing as many Boers as possible. Moving on Lobatsi himself, he despatched Major Bird to Ramathlabama, only fifteen miles from Mafeking, while Col. Bodle, of the B.S.A.P., with 300 of his Police, three Maxims, and a 12½-pounder, penetrated south past Pitsani-Pothlugo without encountering any body of Boers, though three of their scouts were seen to be hastening off in the distance. These men evidently raised an alarm among the besiegers of Mafeking, for Commandant Snyman brought most of his forces from the neighbourhood of the besieged town to resist the intruder, and occupied Pitsani-Pothlugo. Bodle was driven back with a few casualties to Lobatsi, which the Boers proceeded to shell with their 12½-pounder and a pompom. Plumer recalled Bird but, finding Lobatsi difficult to defend, he determined to leave it. Fortunately he had had the foresight to store supplies at Kanya so that now, instead of having to retreat back to Crocodile Pools, he sent off his mounted troops to Kanya, and merely moved his supply base up the line to Crocodile Pools and Gaberones. Next morning the armoured train patrolled the line and discovered that the Boers had been vigorously shelling the deserted positions at Lobatsi, while Plumer himself, with 550 mounted men, two guns and a Maxim were well on their way to Kanya, the remaining 350 men, with two guns were safely laagered at Crocodile Pools.

This manoeuvre left the Boers hopelessly at sea. Nonplussed and distrustful they did not even damage the line above Lobatsi, but retired back again on Mafeking. Plumer, leaving his base at Gaberones, moved forward to Sefetili, thirty miles from the besieged town. On March 26th, he carried out a reconnaissance into the Transvaal nearly as far as Zeerust in order to distract the attention of the Boers, and on the 30th he moved down with 270 mounted men to Ramathlabama. The scouts came into touch with the Boer outposts ten miles north of Mafeking, but the latter retired and the Rhodesians advanced to within five and a half miles of the town before the scouts reported the approach of a large commando. A position was taken up on a ridge and a hot fire at a range of 600 yards was kept up for half an hour. The Boers endeavoured to work round on each flank, but the move was met by a gradual retirement by squadrons, one mounting and taking up a position in the rear while the others covered the movement. For an hour this was carried on steadily, and the Boer fire gradually slackened, the rearguard action proving more deadly to the advancing force than to the Rhodesians. Boer reinforcements pressed heavily on the centre and left flank, but at six o'clock Ramathlabama was reached, and a final desperate rush on the flank was checked by some very fine work from a Police Maxim. The line of retreat was then altered to the right rear, but the Boers did not follow.

The object of the demonstration was fully achieved. The attention of the Boers had been distracted, thus helping the besieged garrison considerably, besides giving them much useful information. The losses, unfortunately, were heavy, amounting to eleven killed, thirty three wounded, and four prisoners. Out of twelve officers, two were killed and four wounded, including Plumer himself. On the conclusion of the engagement at Ramathlabama, the Rhodesians retired to Sefetili without further incident.

CHAPTER TWENTY EIGHT

The Romance of Empire – The Relief Columns Meet – Israel's Farm Mafeking Relieved – The Work of the B.S.A.P. – A British Greeting

During April and May it would have been possible on several occasions for the Rhodesian Column to have made its way into Mafeking, and the proposal was actually made by Plumer, but Baden-Powell thought the risk too great for the little force, especially as the southern column was gradually coming nearer and the garrison still had food for another two months. Plumer, therefore, confined his attentions to the work of harassing the besiegers and thus alleviating the attacks on the town. He was not strong enough to drive the enemy from the vicinity, but his attacks on the Dutch outposts were of vast benefit to the besieged garrison. Reconnaissances in all directions were numerous, and much useful work was done in the direction of assisting the escape of Kaffirs from the town and feeding them.

Occasionally, too, it was found possible to send much needed slaughter cattle into Mafeking. On May 1st, the column, reinforced by 200 of the B.S.A.P. from Mashonaland with an escort of 100 Queenslanders, arrived by a forced march from Beira. Their arrival concluded one of the most romantic phases of any military campaign in history. Coming voluntarily from two widely separated portions of the Empire at the other end of the world, the men had been assembled by long railway journeys, despatched across thousands of miles of ocean to Cape Town, hurried another two thousand miles round the coast to Beira, carried by a narrow gauge railway to Bamboo Creek, changed to a broader gauge at Marandellas, transferred to coaches to Bulawayo, sent on in trains for nearly another 500 miles to Ootsi, and finally given one of the most arduous tasks of the war, marching twenty-five miles a day on foot for four consecutive days, often with no road at all. They arrived, fresh and spirited, just a few hours before they were really badly needed on the field.

On May 14th, Plumer received the glad tidings that Col.

Mahon, with the southern relief column, had got past the Boers and was well on his way to the Malopo River. Plumer at once made a forced march of over 28 miles in 15 hours, and reached Jan Massibi in the early dawn on the morning of the 15th. Here the two relief columns met, and here the men were cheered by the news of an unsuccessful attack on Mafeking made by Eloff three days before. Mahon's column consisted of the Imperial Light Horse (under Col. Edwards, the present C.O. of the B.S.A.P.), the Kimberley Mounted Corps, the Diamond Fields Horse, some Yeomanry, a small detachment of the Cape Police, and 100 volunteers from the Fusilier Brigade, with 'M' Battery, R.H.A., and pom-poms – 1,200 men in all.

Mahon, the senior officer, assumed command of his own and Plumer's columns, and divided them into two brigades under Col. Plumer and Col. Edwards. Marching off early on the 16th, he halted at noon a couple of miles from Israel's Farm, at a point whence Mafeking could be seen for the first time for several months by a free British force. Careful scouting was done and, while the combined column was resting, a detachment of the B.S.A.P., who had been reconnoitring south of the river, galloped back with the report that they had been fired on by Boers from a ridge. These proved to be part of De la Rey's commando of 2,000 men, who had with them, five guns and two pom-poms. The force was posted astride of the Malopo eight miles west of the town, with its centre at Israel's Farm and its left on the ridge where it had been located.

The order was at once given to advance. As the two brigades came into sight the Boer firing commenced. At the farm-house the enemy were making great play with a 12½-pounder and a pom-pom. Col. Bodle and his Police were detached to hold them in check and, if possible, to rid the farmhouse of them. Crossing the river, the Colonel acted throughout the afternoon independently of support. The British right flank was especially assailed, another pom-pom being brought into action in that quarter by the Boers, and the B.S.A.P. had a stiff task before them but, fighting hard against odds, they succeeded in rendering the Boer centre practically impotent. The rest of the Rhodesians were situated on a long ridge on the north bank, their artillery manned by the B.S.A.P. under Capt. Llewellyn. Col. Plumer's left flank comprised the Canadian battery. The South Column, under Col. Edwards, included the I.L.H., and the R.H.A. To the Rhodesians fell the duty of maintaining a fixed position which could hold the main body of the enemy, while Col. Edward's brigade made a direct attack with the object of getting the transport away. This manoeuvre was completely successful, the transport, under Capt. Hook of the Rhodesian Regiment, getting clear through. Towards evening the Fusiliers and a detachment of the Queenslanders reinforced Bodle, who took possession of the farmhouse, at the same time capturing a wagon loaded with ammunition. Firing was continued until after dark but at last the burghers began to fall back, and a general advance completed the rout.

Victorious as he was, Mahon could not be certain that the Boers had not taken up a second position in front of Mafeking, so he ordered his entire army to take up their quarters for the night on the ground they had gained. But later on, hearing from Major Karri Davies, of the I.L.H., who had got safely through to the town, that the coast was clear, he inspanned again in brilliant moonlight and entered Mafeking at half past three on the morning of the 17th. The Boers fled in a panic, not waiting for the pursuit which started some hours later, and left behind them a small gun, some ammunition, some stores, and their papers. After a rest of two days, Plumer's Rhodesians marched to Ramathlabama, ready for the incursion into the Transvaal.

The meeting of Baden-Powell with the young Colonel who had relieved him is interesting as forming one of the most typically British incidents in the whole of the Boer War. Mahon spoke first. 'Glad to meet you. How are you?' he said. 'Good. How are you?' replied the hero of Mafeking. 'It's a long time since we met.' And, happy in the idea that everything had been said that the occasion merited, the two strolled away.

The result of the relief expedition had been waited with breathless interest all over the civilized world. Its success was an almost overwhelming disappointment to the Boers, who were already clamouring in Europe and the United States with demands for intervention. Mahon, the official chief of the relieving force, had indeed done his work well, but the greatest share of the credit must be given to Plumer's men. They had always been outnumbered by their brave and crafty opponents, they had no Imperial troops and very few Imperial officers to stiffen them in one of the most arduous phases of the first year of the War, and they were working all the time on the borders of the enemy's country with wretched guns and constant anxiety about supplies. Yet, by daring tempered with caution, they succeeded in stopping completely any attempt against Rhodesia, and at the same time rendered ineffective some of the strenuous efforts of the Boers to overwhelm the little town of Mafeking. Plumer, like most Commanders, found the good stuff that existed among his officers. As for his men, Police and Volunteers, they proved from the start to be the equals of any troops in the field. Inexperienced, they patiently endured the long delays, the constant and sudden, and sometimes, to them, inexplicable movements up and down the line, and the serious sickness in the malarial country along the Bechuanaland border. Yet on no occasion were they backward in responding to the incessant calls made on them for extra efforts of the highest order. It is difficult with soldiers such as these to single out any for special praise; but at least it may be said that the work of the more experienced B.S.A.P. was never surpassed, not only by their immediate comrades but by any British force of equal numbers throughout the whole sphere of operations. At Bryce's Store, Deerdepoort, Crocodile Pools and in fact, on almost every occasion in which the Rhodesians had been engaged, they had been well to the van, a fact which was tacitly acknowledged when they obtained the post of honour at Israel's Farm. The hardest work of all had fallen on the Police Scouts and outposts, while the gunners of the corps, in their frequent duels with the experts of the 'Staats Artillerie' had done all that was humanly possible with the obsolete guns at their disposal, and had always proved to be a thorn whose sting was not to be eased by the angry burghers. Again the best of the armoured train work had been performed by Capt. Llewellyn and his Police. As Father Hartmann, S.J., the Catholic Chaplain to the Rhodesians, said afterwards, 'But if all the Rhodesians deserve their due share of praise, the B.S.A.P. deserve special mention, the officers as well as the men. Whenever there was hard work at hand, such as a long and fatiguing patrol, forming the advanced guard, and the like, Col. Bodle was called upon to do the work. And he did it always in a soldierly manner.'

Col. Plumer, addressing his column as a whole prior to bidding them farewell, thanked them most heartily for the loyal and unswerving support they had given him throughout the campaign. The War, he said, had been one which would have tried severely the endurance and devotion of any troops and it must have been satisfactory to all ranks of the force to feel that they could look back with pride on the work that had been done, and on the part they had played in the great struggle. He was very proud to have had the honour of commanding the force, and he was sure the services they had rendered were thoroughly appreciated, not only in Rhodesia, but throughout the British Empire.

Addressing the units of the force after the Relief, on May 21st, Baden-Powell said: 'We should have liked to see the Northern Force relieve Mafeking off their own bat. You have not been strong enough to do that, and there will not be much about you in the picture papers, but you have put in seven months of splendid work in a bad country and bad climate. Now you have your reward, for not only have you been able to assist in the Relief of Mafeking, but you have had the honour of bearing the brunt on the right flank of a well fought fight, and have inflicted a severe blow on the enemy, routing him, and kicking him out of Bechuanaland. 'I am proud to command you.' Lord Roberts himself caused to be placed on record his 'high appreciation of the admirable work done by the British South Africa Police, throughout the campaign, during a year of hard work, hard fighting, and often scanty fare.'

CHAPTER TWENTY NINE

Importance and Political Significance of Mafeking
– The Opposing Forces – Preparations for Defence
– The B.S.A.P. take the Post of Honour
– The Wrecking of Capt. Nesbitt's Train
– A Lesson in Dynamite
– Capt. Williams Leads a Punitive Expedition

Mafeking, the 'Place of Stones,' is the typical little market town of South Africa, a 'dorp' of corrugated iron roofs, sociable shaded stoeps, and the big, lazy market place where the outside farmer enjoys his occasional visits by his sleek cattle amid a cloud of pungent tobacco smoke and slow, unimaginative dialogue. It is even a sleepier town than most. Now that the boom of the big guns and the soft whistle of the treacherous shell have vanished from the place, there is nothing more disturbing to be heard than the laughter of the happy nigger, or the creaking of the solemn ox-wagons or the neighing of the sturdy little Basuto pony as he pines for the Home outspan. The only excitement of the week is provided by the passing of the mail train to and from Rhodesia. In one respect it differs from the other little settlements of the Bechuanaland Protectorate, it is British to the core. Half a mile to the south west of the low dagga stores and houses, on either bank of the Malopo River, lie the thickly clustered, thatched huts of a Kaffir town – the most important 'stad' in the district of over a quarter of a million natives. The hard, rocky veldt around, with its scanty cloak of stunted shrubs, is almost unbroken, save for the gorge of the river and a few hillocks to the west of the town.

The place lies on the railway from Cape Town to Rhodesia about 150 miles from Johannesburg as the crow flies, and about 160 from Pretoria. To the former place there runs a good, direct road through Krugersdorp and the Rand. At the time of the siege there was no railway, except the main line, in Bechuanaland or in the Transvaal west of Pretoria. Mafeking, therefore, formed the distributing centre for the British possessions on the west and for the Marico and Lichtenburg districts of the S.

African Republic on the east. There the settlers, Dutch and British, exchange their produce for the manufactured goods which hailed from a distant civilisation. The town was also the centre of the Malmani goldfield. It held important railway shops and stocks, and large quantities of food and forage, stored as a result of the foresight and energy of the well known contractor, Benjamin Weil.

Small and isolated as the place was, it was the only base, in an immense tract of country, where a strong stand of any sort could be made for British prestige. Vryburg, 100 miles to the south, was disloyal, while Kuruman, nearly 200 away, a place of no importance whatever, was held by a hundred or so of the Protectorate Police who had no choice but to surrender during the early months of the war, to an overwhelming host of the enemy. The Boers had no stronger desire than to capture Mafeking. It had formed the starting point for the Jameson Raid, and it had been felt ever since that it might again form the starting point for an expedition against the capital of the Transvaal. Further, it was a most convenient base for any Burgher designs on Kimberley and Cape Colony, or on Rhodesia, while its loss would be a considerable blow to British prestige among the natives of the Protectorate. A British force concentrated here would be useful for any offensive operations that might be launched against the weak western flank of the Transvaal. But the full political significance of the town was not realised until after the fall of Pretoria, when official papers were discovered revealing a most extensive plan which, had it proved successful, might have resulted in a wholesale native war and the final supremacy of the Dutch in South Africa. The fall of Mafeking was appointed as a signal for a concerted rising of the whole of the Dutch in the Cape Colony and Natal. Cronje, no longer engaged in siege work, was to fall on Plumer and crush him with his victorious commandoes, and the Matabele and the Mashonas were to lead their impis to the destruction of the scattered families in Rhodesia, and pave the way for a military alliance with the native tribes from the Zambesi to Table Bay.

It was only at the last moment that a small British force had been thrown into the town. Baden-Powell realised the importance of holding it from the first. Indeed, as was afterwards to be realised by the world, the right man in the young colonel found the right place in the Siege of Mafeking. Only 42 years of age he commanded the 5th Dragoon Guards.

He had already been employed in India, Afghanistan and Ashanti, as well as in South Africa, where he had acted as Assistant Military Secretary and had been chief staff officer to Sir Frederick Carrington during the Matabele rebellion. He knew well the tract of country he was called upon to defend, he was one of the most enthusiastic officers the British Army possessed and he was original in his methods, always encouraging initiative in his officers and in every man of his regiments. He regarded observation and intelligence as two of the most important of all the attributes of a soldier. To defend Mafeking he had not more than 700 or 800 trained soldiers. These were the Protectorate Regiment under Col. Hore, about 470, the B.S.A.P. under Lt.-Col. Walford (90), the Cape Police under Inspectors Marsh and Browne (100), and the Bechuanaland Rifles under Capt. Cowan (70). Fortunately, they were all men accustomed to thinking and acting for themselves in a dangerous country, they were good riders and shots, possessed of the type of mount that was most suitable for the locality, and as a result of their training, they had that extremely valuable quality of 'slimness' which had always been such an acquisition of their burgher foemen. In addition to these there was an extraordinarily reliable volunteer town guard of 400, composed of townspeople, railwaymen, and refugees. Five hundred natives were enrolled for their own protection and to act as cattle guards, watchmen, and scouts. Many more were employed building forts and digging trenches. The white women and children in the town amounted to 650, while there were more than 7,000 natives. The artillery, under Major Panzera of the B.S.A.P., was entirely obsolete, and consisted of four muzzle-loading 7-pounders, with a range of 2,500 yards, a one pounder Hotchkiss, a 2-inch Nordenfeldt, and seven .303 Maxims.

This little force was confronted in the early days of October by one of the largest Boer forces put into the field, which assembled at various camps on the neighbouring border. The Boer estimate gave its numbers as between 9,000 and 11,000 men. Their general was Piet Cronje, one of the most able of the Boer leaders, who was assisted by De la Rey, J.P. Snyman, and Hans Botha. The force – five commandoes in all, crossed the border on the declaration of war and, cutting the line north and south of Mafeking, closed round the town. They had with them two 7-pounders, one 12½-pounder, one 9-pounder Krupp, two quickfiring-¼-pounders and a pom-pom all fitted with a breech-loading action. With these they boasted that they had 'shut up the meercat in his hole.'

The town was an 'open' one, entirely unfortified, but in spite of the ridiculous size of the garrison, the C.O. decided to hold a perimeter of seven or eight miles. The defence was maintained by a series of small forts round the town and the native 'stad'. Sixty works were erected and held in the course of the siege, and the perimeter of the defence was afterwards actually increased to ten miles. It was found that a smaller circle could not keep the town itself out of close rifle range. Each fort was manned with from fifteen to twenty men, provided with two days' food. They were ordered to act on the offensive. As 'B.P.' described it, 'We acted as much as possible on the principle that aggression is the soul of defence, and delivered kicks at the enemy whenever we could with our small numbers find opportunity, and these together with various ruses for shaking the Boer's confidence in themselves, had the effect of toning down any ardour they may have had for attack.'

The armoured train and the railway line protected the most vulnerable north side of the town. The Protectorate Regiment and native levies were responsible for the western defences outside. A squadron of the same regiment was held in reserve. The Cape Police with two Maxims protected the railway line and held Fort Ayr, a detached work on the western defence, the Railway Volunteers garrisoned the cemetery and the adjoining trenches, while to the B.S.A.P. once more fell the post of honour, the holding of the isolated Cannon Kopje, the most commanding height in the outer circle on the south-east. To aid in the defence of this – the key to the whole position – a 7-pounder and two Maxims were posted. The long line of trenches thence to the south-eastern corner of the position was occupied by the 'Black Watch,' or Native Police. Bomb-proof trenches were constructed in the town, look-out towers were built, and telephones installed everywhere to connect with head-quarters. Barricades were piled across the wide streets, and mines were laid in the immediate neighbourhood of the town.

Mafeking was fortunate in its commissariat. There were a large number of cattle in the town, the Protectorate Regiment had six weeks full rations for the men and forage for the horses, and the branch store of Julius Weil & Co. held supplies valued at £30,000. There were other smaller supplies, while large consignments on their way to Bulawayo were found at the station after the cutting of the line.

The B.S.A.P., as was right and proper, were engaged in the first act of war and won much glory therein. Capt. Nesbitt, V.C., had previously escorted a large number of women and children to the south in an armoured train. He was returning with two big guns and a supply of ammunition, sent too late by the authorities at the Cape, after a series of incessant appeals and demands from Baden-Powell. Capt. Nesbitt's train, which consisted of an armoured carriage and a truck, arrived safely at Vryburg on Oct. 11th. A pilot engine, driven by a man named Flowerday, was attached. The fighting force consisted of fifteen men. After a time Flowerday's engine steamed on ahead, to signal back to Nesbitt in the event of things going wrong. At Kraaipan, forty miles south of Mafeking, the engine left the rails. Nesbitt immediately called a halt and his men began to replace them. Up to now there had been no sign of the enemy. Having put the line in order an attempt was made to clear it of the wrecked pilot engine, but there was a heavy load of water in the tank, and they had been working for over half an hour without much result when a bullet flattened itself against the armoured truck. This was followed by a brisk volley. It was dark, and the Britishers had no means of ascertaining the precise direction of the enemy, splinters of lead flew about in all directions, wounding several of the Police and the gallant engine-driver. The pilot engine was unprotected and the water ran out from a hundred holes in her tank. The handful of men continued to work on steadily until the morning.

At daybreak over a hundred Boers were seen sniping from a neighbouring sluit. The Police took to the shelter of the loopholed armoured carriage. They were cheerful and confident and would probably have gained the day against heavy odds, had the Boers not been reinforced. But suddenly, without warning, a dull booming sound was heard and a 40-pound shell dropped near the engine. Even now Nesbitt would not hear of a retreat to Maribogo or Vryburg, but continued the grim fight for another couple of hours in the hope of being relieved by some chance patrol. At last, however, he was wounded, the engine was battered out of all recognition, a white flag was hoisted and the little party surrendered.

The enterprising engine-driver alone escaped. Seeing that the end was near, he slid off the truck on the far side and crawled on his belly for a hundred yards or so in the gutter that ran parallel to the line. Hearing the Boers gallop up to secure their prisoners, he lay prone and, like an ostrich, covered himself as far as possible with sand. On the departure of the jubilant burghers, he crawled for another mile and a half along the gutter and, covering himself once more with sand, slept the untroubled sleep of one who has completed a labour well done. At length he rose and continued his journey, reaching Maribogo tired, dusty, and wounded – but not a prisoner.

The gallant stand of the Police resulted in a loss of two Boers killed and several wounded. Baden-Powell was not slow in retaliating for the reverse that his men had suffered. The town was now completely invested, but on the 13th a party of B.S.A.P. were despatched southwards in an armoured train. Four miles down the line they interrupted a party of Boers who were tearing up the metals. There was a sharp exchange of rifle fire, and the wreckers fled.

On the same day the enemy were taught a sharp lesson, and the garrison were assisted by a good stroke of luck. A couple of truck loads of dynamite stood at the railway station. 'B.P.' was apprehensive lest they might be exploded by a Boer shell and ordered their removal to the veldt at the northern side of the town. A volunteer engine-driver steamed away with instructions to set his trucks loose at the end of a few miles. Six miles along the line he saw Boers in the distance, uncoupling his trucks he gave them a vigorous shunt in the direction of the enemy and returned with his engine. The Boers came to the conclusion that they had intercepted an armoured train and coming within easy range, commenced to pour in a hail of bullets. The result was the explosion of some twenty tons of dynamite. The line was shaken for several miles, the engine driver, now well over a mile a way, thought he was about to be thrown off his engine, and the veldt was strewn with maimed and mangled Dutchmen. The Boers believed the explosion to be intentional and the fact greatly increased their respect for the mines they knew to be laid in the immediate neighbourhood of the town.

On the 14th the armoured train under Capt. Williams of the B.S.A.P. and Railway Volunteers, two Maxims and a Hotchkiss, was despatched to punish some Boers, who had fired on a patrol three miles to the north. Mauser bullets soon began to patter on the trucks and shells dropped perilously near to the train which, however, greatly disconcerted the enemy by its tactics of constantly changing speed, sometimes stopping altogether, and again moving with full steam up. The British guns were doing good work and the Boers kept their distance. After the firing had been continued for some considerable time, 'A' Squadron of the Protectorate Regiment, which had been held in reserve, was sent out from the town in support of their comrades on the train. In their eagerness to get to close quarters with the enemy, they were led too far into the bush country, out of touch with the train. Major Baillie, the correspondent of the *Morning Post*, was despatched by Baden-Powell with a message that 'A' Squadron were to retire at once. Unfortunately, the messenger's horse was hit and he only escaped death by the 'skin of his teeth', and had to seek refuge in the train. Another horseman managed to reach the Protectorate men, only to learn that retirement at that juncture would mean heavy loss and the desertion of the wounded. A gun was then sent out under Lieut. Marchison and 'A' Squadron was enabled to retire on the train. The dead were picked up in the afternoon by a dozen of the B.S.A.P. with a Red Cross ambulance. These men were unarmed but, on approaching the Boers, they were greeted with a hot fire. Cronje afterwards enquired if any of them had been hurt and added that, if so, he would hang by the neck the offending burghers. At last the whole force retired, closely followed by the enemy to within a few miles of the town. The C.O. rode out to meet them, greeting them with a 'Well done, men.' That night an order was issued commending the men of the B.S.A.P. and the Protectorate Regiment for their coolness and courage. Mafeking was greatly elated. The townsfolk saw the stuff their soldiers were made of and noted with delight the reluctance of the enemy to come to close quarters. The British loss was two men killed and one officer and fourteen men wounded.

CHAPTER THIRTY

The Bombardment Begins – 'One Dog Killed' – The Art of Polite Letter Writing – The Attack on Cannon Kopje – Cronje Goes – Life During the Siege – The Manifesto that made Snyman Angry

Cronje's men gradually moved in closer to the town, taking advantage of every rise in the ground not occupied by the garrison. At the end of October one commando lay 5,000 yards south of the town, another camped on the river three miles to the east, a third was three and a half miles to the north east, while Field-Cornet Eloff, the grandson of the President, with a detachment lay west of the 'stad' and various laagers and gun positions were dotted about between the camps.

On the 16th the bombardment commenced with two guns from Signal Hill. Baden-Powell himself has described the event in his book *Sketches in Mafeking and East Africa*. 'I was lucky enough,' he writes,

> to see the first Boer artillery appear on the scene as well as the first shot fired in the investment of Mafeking. It happened that I was looking to Signal Hill, a rise about six miles to the north east where we usually had a lookout post of Cape Police, to my surprise no one was on the hill, but while I looked two or three figures came into view from the far side, and, after an interval of a few minutes, three little groups of men and horses at equal distance appeared on the skyline. They were guns coming into action. A puff of smoke, a distant bang, and a cloud of dust 200 yards away from the town showed that the bombardment had began; but the Boer gunners soon found that the range was too great, and they moved to a nearer position and were thus able to throw their shells into the town.
>
> While watching what effect these were having I turned round and found a lady cycling up the street. I did not know who she was, but I called to her and suggested that

it would be well if she took cover, as the shells were flying about. She said, 'Sorry, but I did not know they were shell', and thanked me very much and rode away rather apologetically, with the air that she had been intruding – not a bit frightened. And that was the spirit of all the ladies, as I soon found out.' Only two shots took effect, both in buildings flying the Geneva cross, the Convent and the Hospital. In the afternoon, General Snyman, who commanded the besieging force that day, despatched a messenger to the town with a white flag. The General's message ran as follows; 'We are here in great force with artillery and we give you a chance to surrender now, to avoid further bloodshed.' 'Bloodshed?' remarked Baden-Powell, with a puzzled expression. 'Ask General Synman when the bloodshed is going to begin. Only one fowl has been killed.' And on Oct. 21st Europe and the World were convulsed with the jocular Colonel's despatch running: 'All well. Four hours' bombardment. One dog killed.'

After the first days' bombardment there was a week's pause in active hostilities. The garrison, directed by Col. Vyvyan and Major Panzera, filled in their time by perfecting the inner defences. The trenches were loopholed, and bomb-proof shelters were provided for almost every house in the town. The women's laager was rendered more secure, and a system of bell signals was improvised by which the townspeople could learn where a flying shell was likely to fall. As the *Times History of the War* states: 'It was not long before those warning bells had become as much a part of the daily routine in Mafeking as the dinner bell is to the ordinary citizen.'

On Oct. 21st the Boers were reinforced by the Scandinavian corps, who brought with them a Creusot breech-loading gun firing a 94lb. shell at an extreme range of 10,000 yards. This was to become known to the people of Mafeking as 'Big Ben,' one of the enemy's smaller guns being more slightingly termed 'Gentle Annie.' Cronje once again summoned the garrison to surrender. He was most anxious to avoid further bloodshed, he declared, and added that there were too many Red Cross flags in the town. There ought only to be one. 'If you bombard the town,' replied 'B.P.', 'You will only create a precedent for our forces when we invade your country. I only ask you to respect the Red Cross on the hospital and convent. You will see a yellow flag floating over one of the town buildings. That building is the gaol. It is chiefly tenanted by your own countrymen, and you can shell it or not, as you please. And by way of thanks for your warning I give you notice that this little town is surrounded by mines, cordite and dynamite. Some go off if you tread on them, others explode when I touch a button in my room. Farewell. My very kind regards and best thanks for your courtesy.' A few shells came from the Boer laager as a guarantee of good faith, and once more the death of a chicken was reported, and a man and a horse were slightly wounded, but beyond this no damage was done.

On the 23rd, a vigorous bombardment was threatened, but the British struck first. Capt. Williams and his B.S.A.P. artillery advanced a couple of guns in the dark to the Waterworks where they shelled the enemy's trenches so effectively as to put two guns out of action. Next day the town was shelled by 'Creaky,' the big Creusot, and some twelve-pounders. The Boers were attempting to damage the railway station but no one was hurt. Again a demand for surrender was made. 'I will let General Cronje know when we have had enough,' was the cheerful reply. On the 25th fire was opened in the early morning from seven guns and an attack on the native town was repelled by the enthusiastic Baralongs, aided by a squadron of the Protectorate Regiment. Two nights later the Boers were driven from their advanced trench on the racecourse by a force of the Protectorate Regiment and the Cape Police.

On the last day of the month Piet Cronje, the General's son, led an attack on Cannon Kopje, the northern outpost held by Col. Walford and forty five of his B.S.A.P. The place was known to the burghers as 'Babiaans' or Monkey Fort, because the garrison had erected a tall iron wind pump as vantage point for the look out man. Cannon Kopje was recognised by both sides as the most important point in the whole position, a point whence a Boer gun would have Mafeking entirely at its mercy, and it had been severely shelled since the start of the bombardment. There was no sort of shell proof cover in the fort, but the men had dug a trench about forty yards in the rear. At the break of day a heavy crossfire from the Boer guns was directed on the kopje, while a host of dismounted burghers were seen advancing through the long grass. As one of the *Red Books* says: 'Before delivering an infantry attack on an entrenched position, first search the trenches well with artillery fire.' But one of the historians of the war has added to this: 'And be very careful to see that the same trenches are not held by a squad of the British South Africa Police'. The men of the B.S.A.P. were indeed, as usual, itching for a real scrap. Col. Walford, who had already taken up a position in front of his men, called for them to leave the trench and man the parapets of the fort. Practically without cover, they opened with their magazines and two Maxims on the enemy who speedily dug a shallow trench whence they directed an incessant rifle fire. Walford was unable to reply to the Boer artillery, for the big guns were over two miles away and he only had a 7-pounder to pit against them. So he reserved his heavier gun for the oncoming infantry. At last it spoke and the attackers broke back to cover, where they continued to snipe at their ease. Time after time the Boers came within charging distance of the fort, but on each occasion they were driven back by the delighted Policemen. A fresh party of Boers were seen advancing more to the south west, to take the fort in the flank. Fire was opened on them from two 7-pounders in the town.

For a time they wavered, halted, and finally fled towards their horses which were held in the rear, followed by their comrades of the frontal attack. Among the wounded was Piet Cronje himself, the leader of the assault. The garrison, still under shell fire, continued their fire at the retreating horsemen as long as they were within range, and then went back to cover at 8.30 a.m. Capt. the Hon. Douglas H. Marsham and Capt. Charles A.K. Pechell, with the two sergeant-majors who took their place, and two troopers, were killed, and five men were wounded, but the Boer loss was far heavier, and the spontaneous praise meted out by the C.O. to the gallant defenders was more enthusiastic than any he had yet given. The official account of the affair remarks: 'Truly did Napoleon rule that in battle a man should never surrender, because he knows not what chance may at the last moment reverse in his favour the most hopeless odds.' The story of Cannon Kopje forms one of the brightest stories in the annals of the Rhodesian Police, as it was the outstanding deed of courage and endurance in that extraordinary series of gallant actions that made the defence of the little town of Mafeking.

Nov. 1st saw the first issue of the *Mafeking Mail-Special Siege Slip*, which was published daily, shells permitting, under the editorship of the correspondent of the *Daily Mail*. Heavy shelling and sniping were now of daily occurrence. On one occasion the Boers tried to imitate the famous dynamite explosion of the first days of the siege, but owing to their clumsy handling of a fuse something went wrong, and the loaded truck blew up a mile and a half from the town, the result being a few mangled Dutchmen.

On the 7th it was learnt that the enemy contemplated another attack on the native town and it was decided to anticipate it by a sortie. Major Godley marched against the western laager with detachments of the Protectorate Regiment and the Bechuanaland Rifles, and three B.S.A.P. guns under Major Panzera. The Boers were surprised and fled for some three or four miles, until their reinforcements had arrived, when Godley retired in good order. He had accomplished his object with a loss of only five men, for the Boers to the west moved some distance further the following night. During the engagement, Major Godley was slightly wounded, and the younger Cronje was killed. The authorities in Pretoria were beginning to feel that General Cronje's reputation as a daring and successful commander was not being maintained, and he certainly showed an exaggerated fear of losing too many lives. There is no doubt at all that had he made a resolute, combined assault with his full strength, Mafeking must have fallen. So on Nov.19th the disgusted General was ordered away to take part in the operations round Kimberley. He took with him three of his largest commandoes and six of the guns. Snyman was left behind with three thousand men, the Long Tom, and four other guns. At the beginning of December two more 5-pounders and a pom-pom were added to the Boer artillery. The investment was not so close as before, the bombardment was less heavy, and the garrison were cheered by the news of three important British successes elsewhere. Much bitterness was felt in the town at the unchivalrous tactics of Snyman who, it was obvious, was deliberately shelling the convent and hospital. However, not much harm was done and, for the most part, the townsfolk settled down to derive as much enjoyment as they could from the conditions of the siege.

Sunday was the great day of the week. A weekly armistice was then regularly observed by both armies. Church services were held by both armies and the advance posts on either side would fraternise. In the afternoon sports of a most ambitious nature would be held. There were polo, cricket and football matches, tent-pegging, pony and bicycle races, and driving competitions for Col. Walford's Police transport mules which always managed to keep in the pink of condition throughout the Siege

– all to the music of an excellent military band. Once a 'Siege Exhibition' was opened. This contained samples of every type of Boer shells, explosive bullets, etc. Another time there was a Baby Show of children born since the commencement of the siege. There were weekly concerts, wherein the C.O. was recognised by everyone as the star performer, with his comic songs and his impersonations. He would imitate Paderewski, a chimney-sweep, or a Mile End coster with equal success, and conclude with a spirited rendering of 'Home, Sweet Home' on a borrowed mouth organ. One verse of a song of his own composition ran as follow:-

> What is the gun
> That makes them run
> When they hear the warning bell?

> You may bet your boots
> It's the gun that shoots
> The high velocity shell.

So the plucky handful of Britishers, stuck in the most desperate plight it was possible for them to conceive, kept up their hearts and saw that the Flag of England remained flying on top of the pole.

The danger of starvation was small, as there were large supplies of food in the town, but there was some grumbling at the restricted allowances, a consequence of Baden-Powell's uncertainty as to the possible end of the siege. He has given the following official account of his arrangements:

> Early in the siege I took over all merchant stocks and put everybody on rations. Beginning on the usual scale, I gradually reduced it to the lowest as would allow of the men being fit for duty. During the latter part of the siege no extras of any kind were obtainable. All lived strictly on the following scale:-

> Meat, at first 1lb., latterly 3/4 to 1lb.
> Bread, at first 1lb., latterly 5 ozs.
> Vegetables, at first 1lb., latterly 6 ozs.
> Coffee, at first 1/3 oz., latterly 1/3 oz.
> Salt, at first 1/2 oz., latterly 1/2 oz.
> Sugar, at first 2 ozs. (latterly none).
> Tea, at first 2 oz. (latterly none).
> Sowens, latterly 1 quart.

We had a large stock of meat, both live and tinned. For live-stock we had to open up a wide extent of grazing ground. We ate the fresh meat first in order to avoid loss from enemy's fire, failure of grass and water, and lung sickness, etc. The tinned meat we stored in bomb-proof chambers and kept as reserve. Our stocks of meal were comparatively small but we had a large supply of forage oats. These we ground down into flour and fermented the residue into sowens (a form of porridge), and the remaining husks went as forage for the horses. Fresh vegetables were largely grown within the defences, and for a greater part of the siege formed a regular portion of the ration.

The cost of feeding the troops was 1/3 a ration, or, with fresh vegetables, 1/6; about 3d. below the contract price in peace. Civilians paid 2/-, and women in the laager 1/2. All liquor was taken over and issued in tots to the troops on wet nights, and I think saved much sickness.

Natives. For the natives we established four soup kitchens, at which horse stew was sold daily, and five sowen kitchens. Natives were all registered, to prevent fraud, and bought rations at one quart per adult, and one pint per child, at 3d. per pint.

Defence watchmen, workmen, police, etc. and certified destitute persons were given free rations. The kitchens so managed paid their own expenses. They were under Capt. Wilson, A.D.C. with Mr. Myers as cash taker and inspector.

The garrison entered with enthusiasm into the work of devising plans for the discomfiture of the enemy. Large megaphones were manufactured, to send bogus orders for the movements of the garrison, greatly misleading the puzzled burghers; dummy forts and dummy trains were erected to draw the Boer fire; a hastily improvised body of lancers were marched round the trenches, well on the sky-line, to make the Boers believe that cavalry reinforcements had arrived. Manifestoes were sent out, 'To the Burghers under arms round Mafeking', saying that the besiegers had been kept in the dark by their own officers. 'B.P.' informed them that the forces at present encountered by their commandoes were only the advance guard of the British Army. 'The main body of the British is now daily arriving from England, Canada, India, and Australia, and is about to advance through the country. In a short time the Republic will be in the hands of the English, and no sacrifice of life on your part can stop it. The question now that you have to put to yourselves before it is too late is – Is it worth while losing your lives in a vain attempt to stop the invasion, or take a town beyond your borders, which if taken will be of no use to you?'

Then followed the shrewd bit. Baden-Powell knew that Boer emissaries in Europe were working hard for foreign intervention. 'The German Emperor,' he wrote, 'is at present in England and fully sympathises with us. The American Government has warned others of its intention to side with England should any power interfere. France has large interests in the goldfields identical to those of England. Italy is entirely in accord with us. Russia has no cause to interfere. The duty assigned to my troops is to sit here until the proper time arrives and then fight and kill until you give in.'

And now a word of advice: 'My advice to you is to return to your homes without delay, and remain peacefully until the war is over. Those who do this before the 13th will, as far as possible, be protected as regards yourselves, your families and property, from confiscation, looting, and other penalties to which those remaining under arms will be subjected when the invasion takes place. Each man must be prepared to hand over a rifle and 150 rounds of ammunition. The above terms do not apply to officers and members of the Staats Artillerie, who may surrender as prisoners of war at any time, nor to rebels on British territory.' Snyman was reminded that he would never capture Mafeking if he simply sat still and looked at it. He became exceedingly angry at the tone of irritating superiority, and the reflections on his skill and courage, and replied with a formal note of protest against the attempt to tamper with his men. Some of his burghers also wrote to Baden-Powell replying that they had received his 'foolish' note with great surprise. 'We have always regarded you as a man of education and patriotism, and also expected you to think the same of us. In conclusion, we wish to inform you that we are perfectly prepared to meet your troops, and that you must therefore let them loose as soon as possible.'

CHAPTER THIRTY ONE

A Reverse – Tpr. Ramsden, V.C. – The uses of a Horse – A Spade War – 'Garrison Cheerful' – Sarel Eloff Arrives for Breakfast and Remains to Dine – The Relief at Last

By this time every able bodied man and woman in the town was working in some way or other for the benefit of the garrison. A traveller for a firm of acetylene gas manufacturers was producing searchlights, the women nursed the sick and made cartridge bags, and the railway men manufactured ammunition and even a 6in. howitzer, which fired an 18lb. shell a distance of 4,000 yards. An eighteenth century Naval gun was unearthed and used with some success. Special issues of stamps and paper money were supplied, and the majority of the natives were employed at trench digging and scouting. Method was shown everywhere. The garrison accounts and the food supply were organised as well as if the times had been normal, a court of summary jurisdiction was set up, and the hospitals were managed most brilliantly with the meagre resources at their disposal. Until Christmas there was nothing further to record. The festival was celebrated with church services, sports, and a bean-feast for the children, and all 'went merry as marriage bell' until the dawn of that fateful 'Black Boxing Day', when the defenders met with their one reverse.

The grazing ground for the cattle had been devastated by locusts and, to keep the animals alive, it was necessary to secure fresh grass at a greater distance from the inner defences. Plumer's column to the north was understood to be approaching Gaberones, and it was thought that an attempt to join hands with him might possibly succeed, and result in the raising of the siege. It was therefore decided to make an attack on Game Tree Fort, a strong position twelve feet high, constructed of sandbags with three tiers of loop-holes. But unfortunately Boer spies were at work and news of the projected sortie reached the besiegers, who doubled the garrison of the fort, and brought up two further commandoes in reserve.

The Police armoured train was instructed to move along the

line to the north, and the attacking force of three guns, two Maxims under Captain Williams, B.S.A.P., and 150 men, with one gun and 110 men in support, to parade at 2 a.m., the right wing being led by Major Godley and the left by Col. Hore, with all the artillery under the command of the B.S.A.P. Officer, Major Panzera. The guns took up a position 1,400 yards southwest of the fort and the armoured train crept out as far as it could go, being stopped at last by the discovery that the line had been destroyed to the left rear of the enemy's work. Abreast of the train, to the right, were the Bechuanaland Rifles, while two squadrons of the Protectorate Regiment advanced along the line to within 200 yards in rear of the train. The guns and the armoured train were to open a heavy cross-fire on the fort at daybreak and continue it until the assaulting party were within 200 yards of the position. A war correspondent in Mafeking has given a vivid account of the start of operations:-

As the grey dawn broke over the veldt we watched anxiously to our left front the spot where we knew our 7-pounders, under Major Panzera, had been emplaced during the night. Then, in the twilight, through the dark green loom of the veldt, broke a flash and a cloud of white smoke. A second later a flash showed bright over the enemy's position, followed by another and yet another, as our two guns came into action, aided by the one at Fort Ayr. Shot after shot fell rapidly round the enemy's position. As it grew lighter, the Maxim joined in, rapping automatically, and to the right the armoured train crept slowly like a great black snake over the plain towards her destination.

The whole scene commenced to unfold itself like a photo which is being developed. The outlines grew sharper. The rattle of musketry broke on our ears and we knew that our men had opened fire and been sighted by the enemy.

After that the attack developed with marvellous rapidity to the east of Game Tree, and Vernon and Fitzclarence took up their positions for a final rush. Away to the right flank, Capt. Cowan, with 70 men of the Bechuanaland Rifles, was disposed to intercept reinforcements or the enemy's retreat. The armoured train under Capt. Williams, with a machine gun and a Hotchkiss, ran up as fast as the broken state of the line would allow. To the left and west of us were the enemy.

Just before the sun rose the armoured train sounded her whistle. It was the signal from Capt. Vernon that he was ready to rush the position and for the guns to cease firing.

But it was fated that victory was not to be ours that day. All the time the big Creusot and the other Boer guns were pouring shells at the British; a misunderstanding had taken place, causing the signal to the British guns to cease fire to sound while the storming party were still 1,200 yards from their destination, and the gunners had failed to dislodge the sand-bags forming the rampart. In the face of a hail of bullets, without a vestige of cover, the attackers rose to their feet and swept on with fixed bayonets, to the foot of the fort. Many fell in the rush. The others, cheering madly as they went, reached the rampart, which they found to be roofed with iron. Two of the officers, in advance, actually fired their revolvers through the loopholes, falling dead on the instant. A corporal gained the roof, and had his clothing shot to rags, but after a few moments all the officers of the regiment were down and most of the men. Slowly the remainder fell back, rallying even under the murderous hail from the fort, but Major Godley had already sent back a despatch running 'The position is practically impregnable to infantry' and Baden-Powell, deciding not to throw away any more lives on an impossible task, ordered a retreat.

Three officers and 19 men were killed, 1 officer and 23 men wounded, and 3 men taken prisoners, as against only 11 Boer casualties. But the action had caused the enemy to marvel. 'These men fight like devils, not men,' they said, and at least the fight proved that the garrison had not lost their old readiness to take the offensive. So impressed were the Boers that they dared not follow up their advantage, and it was afterwards learnt that they would have surrendered but for one man, who had threatened to shoot the first burgher showing the white flag.

Two men of the Protectorate Regiment won the right to wear the V.C., during the engagement. One of them, Tpr. H.E. Ramsden, shortly afterwards transferred to the B.S.A.P. He had carried his wounded brother from the very edge of the trenches to the protection of the 7-pounder.

Still the long and weary weeks dragged on. After their reverse the garrison were constantly expecting an attack in force, but the Boers were filled with a wholesome dread of the numerous imaginary mines that 'B.P.' had warned them against, and they kept their distance. News of the defeats at Colenso and Stormberg reached Mafeking, to add to the general feeling of depression. One day in January a Krupp gun arrived from Pretoria which started its active career by killing two little children in the women's laager, and at length typhoid broke out amongst the non-combatants.

But none of the devoted band lost heart. The Naval Gun 'Lord Nelson' was mounted on a carriage extemporised with the aid of a pair of wagon wheels, round-shot was manufactured, and the gentle Nuns at the Convent made three-pound cartridges under the direction of Major Panzera. It was found that the old gun could throw a ball a distance of over 3,000 yards, and henceforth it helped the defenders considerably, while the home made howitzer was regarded by the Boers as a weapon that had found its way by miraculous means into the town.

At the end of January, only sufficient food remained for seventy-seven days. However the Baralongs raided many of the Boer cattle from the laagers, and there was always horse-flesh to fall back upon. 'B.P.' Had related some of the divers extraordinary uses of a horse in *Sketches in Mafeking and East Africa*: 'The manes and tails,' he writes, 'went to fill mattresses at the hospital, the hide, after having the hair scalded off, was boiled with the head and hoofs to make brawn; the meat was cut off and minced; the interior arrangements were cut to lengths and used as sausage skins for the mince (a ration was six-inches of sausage); the bones and shreds of meat were boiled into soup, and the bones were then collected and powdered into dust and used for adulterating the flour.

About this time news of British victories in the South arrived and, on Feb. 11th, a message was received holding out hopes that the town would be relieved in May. Shortly afterwards the Boers began to be aggressive in the neighbourhood of the brickfields on the south-east. They were rapidly pushing their trenches nearer to the town, and a war of spades began. The Britishers began to cut a series of parallels, connecting works, and sapping trenches towards the Boer entrenchments. The sappers were protected from rifle fire by loop-holed steel shields. On March 2nd, less than thirty yards separated the trenches of the combatants. That night the Boers attempted to dislodge the garrison by flinging dynamite bombs. Immediately a sergeant devised a plan for retaliating more effectively with the aid of a fishing rod, which was most successful in throwing grenades and bombs manufactured from fruit tins. On the same day the home-made howitzer dislodged the Creusot, which was moved to the south-east heights, whence it was moved once again, after its gunners had been picked off by snipers. Sniping at close quarters was now continuous and deadly. On the 8th the garrison was cheered by news of Cronje's surrender at Paardeberg on Majuba Day, and copies of the *Mafeking Mail*, announcing the event were wrapped round large stones and fired from the cannon into the enemy's camp. This was followed by the great tidings of the relief of Ladysmith and Kimberley, and the British spirits were as excellent as the Boers were depressed. On the 22nd native runners announced that Plumer was only twenty-four miles away.

On the following night the Boers, apparently surfeited with the constant sniping and the fighting at close quarters, left the trenches at the brickfields in silence, and in the morning they were occupied by the cheering Britishers. Mafeking was once again out of range of rifle fire and her guns could reach the Boer laagers once more. Shelling was now spasmodic. On some days it was continued incessantly, while on others hardly a shot was fired. The eastern Boer trenches were gradually evacuated.

On April 1st, the burghers sent in an 'April Fools' message to the effect that Plumer had been routed with heavy loss. On the 3rd Baden-Powell learnt that he had actually been forced to retire after heavy skirmishing, and came to the conclusion that relief could not arrive until the relieving force had been strengthened.

The Baralongs now began to stream out of the town past the Boer pickets, to seek supplies and protection from Plumer's column, and at the end of the siege the garrison had 1,300 fewer mouths to feed. Thirty-one of the unfortunate Kaffirs were captured and massacred, while a party of women were flogged almost to death, and driven back into the town.

England was praying against hope that her gallant children could hold out for just a little longer, and the most confirmed cynics were calling in their hearts for the aid of some miraculous power, but their anxieties were wasted. This was the message despatched to Lord Roberts on May 7th, two hundred days and one week after the commencement of the siege: 'All going well; fever decreasing; garrison cheerful; food will last till about the 10th June.' These were spirits that no hardship could break. And yet matters were not in reality going well with them at all. The cold season was imminent and there was a scarcity of fuel; nearly all the trees in the lines of defence having been converted into fuel long before. The medical stores were nearly exhausted. The repeated rumours of relief had not been verified, and were now discredited altogether, and as a last straw Lord Roberts sent word late in April that if Baden-Powell had not yet joined hands with Plumer, the town must be prepared to make supplies last even longer than he had previously stated.

But the tide turned at last. At the end of the second week in May, the big Boer gun was hurried away to Pretoria, a sign that the burghers were giving up their hope of capturing the town, and at last it was announced that relief was actually in sight and that the siege would not last longer than another two or three days. But Commandant Eloff, Kruger's grandson, a more venturesome Boer than most, had resolved to make one final desperate attempt against the 'rooineks.'

He even posted up in the Boer laager a notice stating: 'To-night we set out for Mafeking. To-morrow morning we Breakfast in Dixon's Hotel.' The valiant Eloff had only recently returned from a visit to the President who had ordered him to take Mafeking at all costs. He had repeated the instruction to Snyman, pointing out that the relieving columns were rapidly advancing, Hunter was already across the Vaal, and Carrington had landed at Beira with men and guns. It would be cowardly to sit down any longer. Snyman consented to the undertaking with reluctance and, in the event of Eloff entering the town, promised his support. Eloff was to take with him a force of 700 men, capture the B.S.A.P. fort on the south-west of the town and, having gained that point of vantage, await the reinforcements for the final assault on the town itself. But the Boers never cared over much for direct attack, entailing hand to hand fighting, for no more than 225 men, for the most part foreign mercenaries, presented themselves at the rendezvous on the morning of the 12th. Eloff, however was determined and set out with his band along the sunken bed of the Molopo, while

Snyman was supposed to be making a pretended assault upon the east. The young leader fired the 'stad' without resistance. This should have been the signal for the advance of Snyman with reinforcements but the craven general thought better of the plan and decided to desert his colleague. At four in the morning heavy firing was heard in the eastern trenches, but it was seen to be too stationary to be anything but a blind, and warnings were sent to the British detachments elsewhere. Shortly afterwards flames were seen piercing the darkness from the direction of the native village, accompanied by rifle firing and cheering. The inner line of defences was penetrated for the first time in the history of the siege. Three hundred Boers had got through, in spite of the plucky resistance of the surprised Baralongs. The garrison was now thoroughly aroused. Alarm bells were sounded in every direction. Everyone in the town was hastily armed, even the prisoners in the gaol, who loyally assisted in the defence with the utmost enthusiasm. Small but eager boys were utilised as despatch bearers and women gladly hastened to carry coffee and provisions to the garrison and to nurse the wounded under fire. There was no confusion, and each man fell in at his appointed place without a word. Never had the spirits of the townspeople reached so high a pitch, 'and they began to look upon the affair as a sporting event' – especially when they found that the commissariat were serving them during the fighting with the most generous meal they had tasted for weeks.

Eloff pushed on to the B.S.A.P. fort, a one storey building held by Col. Hore and fifteen of the Protectorate Regiment. A single volley would have blown them all to pieces, and resistance was hopeless. One man, told to throw down his rifle, replied, 'I'll see you damned first!' He fell dead with five bullets through him and the Boers occupied the fort. A burgher telephoned to headquarters: 'We are Boers. We have taken Mafeking.'

But he was mistaken. Eloff had come into the town, but the next point that arose was how he was going to get out. The Boers, some still in the 'stad' and the remainder in the Police fort, were already separated by the Protectorate Regiment, while the Cape Police with a Maxim held Snyman at bay, and the fort itself was surrounded by all the troops available. The native town was shelled by a 7-pounder and then overcome by means of a stirring bayonet charge. Eloff held out gallantly till the evening. His men had demanded instant surrender, and

Eloff had fired his revolver into the crowd, taunting them with cowardice. But at 6 o'clock, seeing that his water tanks were perforated with bullets and water was unobtainable, he approached his prisoner, Hore, and handing over his weapon, said, 'I surrender to you, sir.'

At the meeting of Eloff and Baden-Powell, the Englishman softened, as best he could, the bitterness of his gallant enemy's defeat. 'Good evening, Commandant,' he added, 'Won't you come in and have some dinner?' So Sarel Eloff came into Mafeking for breakfast and remained to dine, and rumour has it that he was as valiant a trencherman as he was a fighter. The jubilant British rifle-men went back to their horseflesh with renewed appetite, while the prisoners who had been released for the engagement handed back their rifles and bandoliers to the warders and went back to gaol.

Eloff was plied with the choicest viands the town possessed. He had much to say of the cowardly Snyman, 'But whose blood I will have some day. You must be taken, Colonel.' 'B.P.' suggested that possibly Lord Roberts or somebody would hear that he was besieged, and send a force to relieve him some day. 'I know all about that relieving force,' responded the still confident Eloff, 'It set out several days ago from Kimberley and is marching parallel with the railway. But we shall smash it at Koodoos Rand.'

Such was the fitting end of the immortal siege. Four days later a carrier pigeon arrived from Col. Plumer with the news that the two relief columns had started at daybreak. Shortly after 1 o'clock in the afternoon, shells were seen bursting seven miles away and the Boers were noted to retire before the advancing British. At 4 p.m. came the heliograph message: 'From Col. Mahon's force, how are you getting on?' The reply was the one word: 'Welcome.' The feeble survivors among the horses were gathered together, and a few mounted men with two B.S.A.P. guns set out to demonstrate in Mahon's direction. At 6 o'clock the relief column was only six miles from the town and at 7 p.m. Major Karri Davis, I.L.H, with ten men marched into Mafeking.

The Major informed the first man he met in the town that he and his men were a part of the relief force. 'Are you, by gad?' exclaimed the man of Mafeking and, in a few minutes, the wild cheering of the townsfolk almost amounted to a frenzy, as the war worn troopers of the Light Horse rode through the crowd. The rest of the column arrived at 4 o'clock next morning.

CHAPTER THIRTY TWO

'Mafficking' – Roberts enters Pretoria
– 'B.P.' and Plumer in the Western Transvaal
– The Storm Bursts – 'I Propose Holding Out'
– 'B.P. prepares for Another Siege'
– The Salvation Army brings Relief – A Tight Corner
– B.S.A.P. to the Rescue

The news of the relief reached the fast beating heart of the Empire on the night of May 18th. Thousands of people had poured into London from the provinces, in the hope that they might be among the first to hear the glad tidings. All day long they had besieged the War Office, but the placard bearing the inscription 'No News' had been the only message to greet their anxious eyes. Then at last, in the stop-press column of the last edition of the *Evening News*, printed on this occasion some minutes before time appeared the following: 'Relief of Mafeking – Mafeking has been relieved – Food has entered the Garrison – Enemy dispersed' – Reuter.

In a moment, England cast aside the reputation for a lack of outward emotion that had clothed her for centuries in the eyes of the world, and the cue was given to the Empire to enter on one period of genuine temporary insanity her history has known. The theatres emptied simultaneously and the streets of the Metropolis were filled, apparently from nowhere, with a dense crowd of ecstatic, laughing, shouting humanity.

Union Jacks were flown in thousands, every man in uniform to be seen was hoisted aloft above the heads of the multitude, and stolid City merchants left the shelter of their hansoms to gain the roofs of the vehicles whence their shouting could be heard the better. A myriad hats changed heads, grave dignitaries of the Church condescended to exchange salutes with the merry coster-girls who tickled their chins with long 'fevvers' bought for the occasion; and so for more than two days the business of the Empire was at a standstill, and this emotion that had gripped the British world for so many weary months surged out in mad, glad flood of irresponsibility. The word

'Mafficking' was created to express a symptom of the British temperament hitherto unknown, and it is more than possible that, to the historian, the little border township in the veldt will best be known as the source whence a new word was added to the vocabulary of the English language.

The Queen alone kept her dignity unassailed. This was the message she wrote at her dinner table with her own hand to 'B.P.' and his proud little following immediately on receipt of the great news:-

> I and my whole Empire greatly rejoice at the relief of Mafeking, after the splendid defence made by you through all these months. I heartily congratulate you and all under you, military and civil, British and native, for the heroism and devotion you have shown. – V.R. and I.

In the course of Lord Roberts' official despatch, occurred this magnificent tribute to the B.S.A.P. and the other gallant Colonials who had kept the flag flying:-

> No episode in the present war seems more praiseworthy than the prolonged defence of this town by a British garrison, consisting almost entirely of Her Majesty's Colonial forces, inferior in numbers and greatly inferior in artillery to the enemy, cut off from communication with Cape Colony, and with the hope of relief repeatedly deferred until the supplies of food were almost exhausted.

Baden-Powell himself, after complimenting the various units of his little army, on the cessation of the siege, especially congratulated Major Panzera and his Police gunners on their cool shooting, and the way they had stuck to their guns with weapons either obsolete or home-made. To the B.S.A.P. as a whole he gave an almost silent tribute which was more effective than any other he had framed. They needed no eulogy, he said, for they were 'the defenders of the little red fort on the hill that Cronje could not take.'

The regiment had indeed played the most manful part of all in the Great Siege, which had at least proved to the world what could be accomplished in war by ingenuity and courage. Ten thousand Boers had been rendered useless during the most critical month of the campaign and never less than two thousand during the whole seven months of the siege. The British loss was no more than 35 killed, 101 wounded and 27 prisoners, while the Boer losses amounted to over 300. On the relief of Mafeking, Kruger realised for the first time that his cause was a lost one, and on May 29th, he left Pretoria in a hurry, taking with him some ten million pounds sterling, the property of the Transvaal Republic. Lord Roberts entered Pretoria with his victorious army on June 4th.

It seemed now as though the end of the war was in sight, but it was apparent even to the most confident that much yet remained to be done. In the south and east of the Transvaal the enemy were unbroken, in the Free State the commanders of the various British columns had their hands full, while Buller was faced with a large force of burghers on the Drakensberg. Louis Botha himself remained at the head of the main Dutch columns only a few miles from the capital. Soon the lines of communication were threatened by a series of Boer successes in the Free State.

Negotiations for peace were futile, and the great achievements of that remarkable guerrilla, Christian De Wet, on the railway line revived the fading spirits of the burgher troops and brought back hosts of waverers into the field in all parts of the country. At Diamond Hill, Roberts removed the most pressing menace to the capital, but De la Rey managed to cross over undisturbed and stir up fresh trouble in the Western Transvaal.

Baden-Powell was ordered to occupy Zeerust and then start east with such of his following, relievers and relieved, as were fit for the field. With him marched the B.S.A.P. of the garrison, and of Plumer's force; there were also the Rhodesian Volunteers, a battery of Canadian artillery, and three other guns. 'B.P' continued his march to Rustenburg: without halt, accepting the surrenders of tired Boers and collecting arms and ammunition en route. It is said that many scores of Snyman's men travelled miles to behold the man who had repulsed their assaults on Mafeking, held their finest leaders in derision, and finally captured 200 of their bravest troops. At Rustenburg a halt was made. Baden-Powell was entrusted with the subjugation of the Marico district, one of the fairest pieces of territory in S. Africa, studded with smiling farms, and orange groves, and well-watered pastures. Garrisons were left at Mafeking, Ottoshoop, Lobatsi and Zeerust. Lord Edward Cecil was left to administer the district, and Baden-Powell continued on his way to Pretoria, to receive his instructions in person from

Lord Roberts. He was now ordered to pacify the district north of the Magaliesberg and move to Warmbads, in conjunction with a brigade of Carrington's Imperial Bushmen, who brought up his total force to about 3,000.

But there were stupendous difficulties in the way of the light-hearted hero of Mafeking. In the deep ravines and recesses of the Magaliesberg Mountains there was no lack of supplies for the commandoes, whose wives and children lay in perfect seclusion in a thousand kloofs that had never known a British soldier, while there were no richer valleys than the district provided for the growing of crops in the whole of the Transvaal. De la Rey, the finest of all the Boer generals, assumed command and he had brought with him not Krupps, which would require ammunition from headquarters, but British 15-pounders, which he hoped to keep supplied by helping himself from British convoys. His forces consisted of 7,000 men, with 12 guns, four pom-poms and three Maxims.

But throughout the whole of June the burgher preparations in the west had been kept secret. Baden-Powell had seemed perfectly immune from attack, indeed he had been principally occupied in chastising unruly Kaffirs in the Pilandsberg and organising a service of private transport through his district. Roberts came to the conclusion that he could be withdrawn with safety to the north of Pretoria, so he ordered him to evacuate Rustenburg and occupy Commando and Zilikats Neks, two of the half-dozen practicable passes that penetrate the Magaliesberg, preparatory to the move North.

Then the storm burst. The garrison of Rustenberg, eighty men with a gun, under Lord Edward Cecil, inspanned and proceeded to trek on the morning of July 4th. In obedience to orders, they moved at top speed until midday on the 5th, when a despatch rider dashed up to the column with a message that Rustenberg was in danger and the whole force was to hurry back, before the Boers could occupy the town and dominate the district. This was utterly impossible, but it so happened that the garrison had met on the road with two squadrons of Australian bushmen and a field gun, under Capt. McKattie. These volunteered to push back and hold the town against all comers.

But Rustenberg was still safe. Baden-Powell hearing of the danger, had despatched Major Hambury-Tracy with 120 B.S.A.P. to the probable scene of action. They arrived on the 5th just in time. On the following day Commandant Limmer, with the Marico and Lichtenberg commandoes, surrounded the town and demanded unconditional surrender. They had with them a Maxim and a field gun. Now on the previous day the gallant major had received an order from Pretoria to evacuate the place, but he now replied that in his opinion a retirement would be most impolitic, and added 'I propose holding out.' And his B.S.A.P. who had just emerged from the longest siege of the century, were with him to a man. So the morning of the 6th found them occupying a series of positions round the town. The gaol, which was the soundest position in the place, was well garrisoned.

Rustenberg contained the country home of Kruger and held a more than strong glamour of sentiment for the burghers of the district who made up Limmer's fighting force. These were said to be the best shots and the finest fighters in the Transvaal. They had been the first to meet the grim warriors of the Lancashires at Spion Kop, and they had assisted in the great assault on Ladysmith in January. So was the little garrison of Policemen hard pressed.

The battle started at sunrise on the 7th. The gaol was peppered briskly by the spiteful Boer with Maxim, and the sharp-shooters on both sides settled down to an extraordinary rifle duel which lasted for six hours without either side gaining any advantage. At eleven o'clock a clatter of hoofs and a wild 'cooee' were heard and a welcome squadron of McKattie's Bushmen rode at a gallop into the town, while the other squadron with the field gun dashed across the plain to take up a position to the south.

For a few minutes the burghers greeted the newcomers with a shower of lead, but the surprise had been too great for their 'slim' nerves and they fled at last, with the 12-pounder spitting shells at them, and B.S.A.P. and Bushmen racing after them in hot pursuit at the fastest pace their horses could show. Rustenburg was saved. Though beaten, Limmer was able to seize the important pass over the Magaliesburg, where he established communication with another strong Boer column and forced Baden-Powell to hurry back to Rustenburg, which was reinforced by Plumer's command. Here, though only sixty miles away from the headquarters of Lord Roberts' victorious army, the British commander was compelled to stay for almost a month. The whole countryside had risen after the unfortunate evacuation of Rustenburg on the 4th, and in every direction lay swarms of burghers – some of the best shots in the world, who rode mounts suitable to the locality and who knew every inch of their district. At Zilikats and Commando Neks a strong force of Scots Greys and R.H.A. was captured by De la Rey, and 'B.P' was obliged to sit tight and prepare for another siege. He fortified the hills surrounding the town, mounted guns on them, dug shelter trenches and erected bomb-proof shelters. All the food stuffs available were gathered together and the troops were put upon half rations.

But the investment broke at its commencement. Methuen who had been doing great work in the north of the Free State, had been hastening northward through the disturbed districts and now made for the storm centre at Rustenburg with his famous 'Salvation Army,' as it had come to be called. On the 21st, he arrived at the pass of Olifant's Nek, which he found to be held by the Boers. His artillery cleared the lower ridges of the position and four battalions of infantry, after a stubborn resistance lasting four hours, drove the burghers from the Nek. Communication was thus established with Rustenburg, but the victory was not as decisive as it should have been. 'B.P.' was, for once, too cautious. Not caring to take the risk of leaving Rustenburg, he made but a half-hearted attempt to cut off the retreat of the Boers, who should have been annihilated. Instead, they got away with their horses, their guns, and every one of their wagons.

Methuen was ordered south again to put a stop to an outbreak of train wrecking on the Potchefstroom line. Before leaving, however, he garrisoned Olifant's Nek with the Loyal North Lancashires, under Col. Kelsewick of Kimberley fame. Then on July 23rd, Baden-Powell was again left to himself and De la Rey had full opportunity to attack his isolated detachments.

The first force to come into action was a column of 300 Bushmen under Col. Airey, who had gone to fetch in a convoy from Elands River. They were surrounded, all their horses were stampeded and shot, and they lost six killed and nineteen wounded before help arrived. After fighting all day without guns, in the teeth of an ambuscade as ugly as it was possible to devise, they were relieved by the Protectorate Regiment, under Capt Fitzclarence and a detachment of B.S.A.P., who finished the rout with a cross country gallop after the panic-stricken burghers.

A fortnight later, this engagement was followed by the very serious attack at Elands River, where a force of Imperial Bushmen and Rhodesians, under Col. Hore, put up a resistance which has been sung by most of the historians of the war as the finest deed of arms of the whole campaign. The Rhodesians were led by Major Hooper of the B.S.A.P. who held a command at the time with the Rhodesian Volunteers. Fortunately a handful of straggling units of the Police had managed to find their way to the side of the 200 Rhodesians before the action commenced and so were enabled to share in the most extraordinary stand against overwhelming odds that Colonial troops have yet provided.

APPENDIX ONE

THE SOUTH AFRICAN WAR

A brief narrative of the part taken by the B.S.A.
Police in the South African War 1899 – 1902.
By: Lieut. Col. A.J. Tomlinson

Soon after the outbreak of hostilities in 1899, Capt. Hoel Llewellyn was sent in an armoured train with a maxim gun and a detachment of the B.S.A. Police into Bechuanaland; this was the means of preventing the Boers from advancing beyond Gaberones; further detachments were sent by train to the South as operations increased.

Col. Plumer commanded the forces from Southern Rhodesia, and there were several engagements with the enemy in which the B.S.A. Police took part; finally Plumer formed a military camp at Sefetili (Bechuanaland) in April 1900, to await an opportune time to relieve Mafeking, which was being heavily attacked. With Plumer's troops were three squadrons of B.S.A. Police under Capt. Bowden (with Lieuts. Bateson and McGee), Capt. Nesbitt, V.C. (with Lieuts. Moore and Howes), and Lieut. Tomlinson (with Lieuts. Wood and Godley), the whole commanded by Lieut. Col. Bodle.

On 15 May Plumer started with his whole column for Mafeking, meeting on the way a column from the South under Col. Mahon. It is well-known that the combined forces were victorious, and the enemy was defeated after somewhat severe fighting, and Mafeking was relieved on 17 May 1900.

No time was then wasted, and the B.S.A. Police, under Col. Bodle, were soon on the march into the Transvaal, making for Rustenburg, where operations were conducted for some time in the district: the B.S.A. Police were allotted positions on the hills surrounding the town, and it was not long before fighting took place with a Boer commando from the South; this was driven off, and a fierce fight took place soon afterwards at Warmbaths, whence Plumer's forces pursued another commando, which was repulsed and which then retired. A part of Plumer's troops at Rustenburg consisted of an Australian regiment which, whilst on patrol one day, was trapped in a hilly pass some thirty miles from the town. When the news came in, the B.S.A. Police under Col. Bodle were immediately detailed to go to the 'Aussies" assistance. With the arrival of this force, the enemy retired, but had inflicted a loss of nineteen killed and many wounded of the Australians, with a number of horses captured, before the B.S.A. Police got to the pass.

And so it went on from day to day, fighting when the enemy was encountered.

As the Rustenburg district became fairly quiet, Col. Plumer's force moved towards Pretoria and took up a position near the M'silikatzi Pass, in the Magaliesburg Range. Here the B.S.A. Police were sent, with other detachments in turn, on daily patrols; guerilla warfare was now the order of the day in the surrounding country.

Some time elapsed and then news came through that Pretoria had been taken by Lord Roberts on 4 June, whereupon the B.S.A. Police, with the rest of Plumer's column, marched to the Transvaal capital and were camped just outside the town. Although it was considered that the Boers would now give in altogether, it was soon found that they intended to carry on with guerilla tactics, so 120 B.S.A. Police (under Major Hanbury Tracey) were again sent to Rustenburg. Shortly after, the garrison was surrounded by a superior enemy force, and but for the timely arrival of reinforcements of a detachment of an Imperial regiment, would undoubtedly have had to capitulate. On another occasion the Australian regiment on patrol was again surrounded near a place called Eland's River, when thirty nine men were killed or wounded, and many horses shot or stampeded, and but for Capt. Fitzclarence with the Protectorate regiment and a detachment of B.S.A. Police coming to the rescue, our force must have surrendered.

The B.S.A. Police took part in various minor operations at this time, and eventually were released from service and returned to Southern Rhodesia in December 1900.

But the anticipated conclusion of hostilities did not come about, and so, on 27 September 1901, Major Drury, with Lieuts.

Chapman and Ingham, with one hundred and twenty five N.C.O.s and men, left Bulawayo for Mafeking and joined Lord Methuen's column; A further twenty five men under Lieut. Agar were also sent South in February 1902.

An unfortunate occurrence happened when a British convoy of Methuen's column was captured in February 1902. The detachment of B.S.A. Police, under Lieut. Ingham, was escort to the guns on this occasion and fought for nearly three hours, and did not surrender until completely surrounded. The officer in charge of the guns afterwards wrote to Col. Bodle in high terms of the gallantry of the B.S.A. Police.

Major Drury's detachment of the B.S.A. Police continued with the Imperial troops until the conclusion of the war in May 1902.

The foregoing is merely an outline of the services rendered by the B.S.A. Police in the South African War. It should be placed on record that His Majesty King Edward VII was pleased to mark his appreciation of the services of the B.S.A. Police by the presentation of Colours to the Corps, which are valued exceedingly.

The Outpost
December 1940

In a telegram dated 19 November 1900, to Col. Bodle, British South Africa Police, Bulawayo, the Military Secretary, Chief Army Headquarters, Johannesburg, stated:

The British South Africa Police, having left Pretoria to return to their regular duties, the Field Marshal Commander-in-Chief desires to place on record his high appreciation of the admirable work done by the Corps throughout the campaign. Lord Roberts much regrets he was unable to see the British South Africa Police before they left his command, and requests that you will accept yourself and convey to officers, non-commissioned officers and men, how much he valued the gallant service they have rendered during the past year of hard work, hard fighting and scanty fare.

APPENDIX TWO

Nominal Roll of members of the British South Africa Company's Police attested from 24 November 1889 to 12 September 1890

Attested from
24.11.89 to 12.9.90

"A" Troop

Officers

Lieut-Col PENNEFATHER, EG
Captain WILLOUGHBY, Sir John C
Captain HEYMAN, HM
Paymaster MOLYNEUX, W
Lieutenant CAPPER, O
Lieutenant GRAHAM, MD
Medical Officer RAND, RF
Medical Officer GOODY, E
Sub-Lieut FIENNES, The Hon Eustace W

NCOs and Men

No	Rank	Name	Date Attested
201	TSM	STANLEY, G	15.2.90
202	Sergeant	HARRIS, TH	15.2.90
205	Sergeant	PAXTON, T	15.2.90
456	Sergeant	HICKEY, R	31.3.90
473	Sergeant	BROWN, H	31.3.90
203	Corporal	MCMULLIN, J	15.2.90
206	Corporal	NEWBOLT, KD	15.2.90
216	Corporal	LEVITT, S	17.2.90
257	Corporal	BAILEY, D	20.2.90
286	Corporal	SEYMOUR, S	21.2.90
288	Corporal	KENNEDY, H	21.2.90
291	Corporal	VAISEY, SW	22.2.90
299	Corporal	CARTER, AJ	21.3.90

213	Lance Corporal	HURLEY, J	15.2.90
289	Lance Corporal	DORNING, HB	21.2.90
452	Farrier	GODWIN, A	11.3.90
180	Trooper	BLUNDELL, A	28.1.90
204	Trooper	BROWNE, WH	15.2.90
207	Trooper	KING, BS	15.2.90
209	Trooper	PHILLIPS, A	15.2.90
210	Trooper	WILLIMITE, W	15.2.90
211	Trooper	CURTOIS, F	15.2.90
212	Trooper	LAING, R	15.2.90
214	Trooper	HALLBERG, G	15.2.90
218	Trooper	BRAND, C	17.2.90
220	Trooper	KOPPING, A	17.2.90
222	Trooper	DYAS, W	17.2.90
223	Trooper	FRASER, W	17.2.90
225	Trooper	ORPEN, C	17.2.90
227	Trooper	MULLIGAN, J	17.2.90
229	Trooper	BARBER, GG	17.2.90
233	Trooper	GRAY, JP	17.2.90
234	Trooper	ENRIGHT, T	20.2.90
236	Trooper	KOESTER, H	20.2.90
258	Trooper	MITCHELL, J	20.2.90
261	Trooper	BRITTON, J	20.2.90
262	Trooper	JONES, J	20.2.90
263	Trooper	FORREST, W	20.2.90
265	Trooper	KELLEY, PC	20.2.90
266	Trooper	FRIEND, G	20.2.90
267	Trooper	BIRNEY, J	20.2.90
268	Trooper	HUGHES, E	20.2.90
269	Trooper	REDMOND, H	21.2.90
270	Trooper	FINCH, GH	21.2.90
271	Trooper	OSBORNE, G	21.2.90
272	Trooper	COCHRANE, JH	21.2.90
273	Trooper	MARCUS, S	21.2.90
275	Trooper	GROTJOHN, G	21.2.90
277	Trooper	JOLIFFE, W	21.2.90
278	Trooper	BLOCK, W	21.2.90
279	Trooper	ZEIGENBEIN, C	21.2.90
280	Trooper	MCLACHLAN, C	21.2.90
281	Trooper	ALLAN, J	21.2.90
284	Trooper	GREEN, W	21.2.90
287	Trooper	CLAYTON, F	21.2.90
290	Trooper	BAXTER, T	21.2.90
292	Trooper	CARTER, AW	22.2.90
294	Trooper	DOVETON, W	22.2.90

No	Rank	Name	Date
295	Trooper	GLASS, GWC	22.2.90
297	Trooper	AURET, WH	22.2.90
298	Trooper	NEWITT, H	22.2.90
300	Trooper	BOLTE, A	22.2.90
373	Trooper	FOOTE, J	27.2.90
379	Trooper	MCMULLIN, S	27.2.90
447	Trooper	KRAUSE, C	22.3.90
448	Trooper	MATTHEWS, T	11.3.90
449	Trooper	FARMANNER, H	11.3.90
450	Trooper	BARRINGTON, W	11.3.90
451	Trooper	GLOVER, TW	11.3.90
453	Trooper	CREIGHTON, CF	22.3.90
470	Trooper	BROWN, T	31.3.90
476	Trooper	TILNEY, J	31.3.90
497	Trooper	AYLEN, J	24.4.90
498	Trooper	NICHOLLS, JE	24.4.90
499	Trooper	VINNEY, J	24.4.90
500	Trooper	WHITE, TW	24.4.90
505	Trooper	LOUW, JG	30.4.90
506	Trooper	O'HARA, B	30.4.90
512	Trooper	GREY, T	3.5.90
514	Trooper	CARNEY, B	4.5.90
528	Trooper	GRAHAM, H	14.5.90
530	Trooper	HANNAY, WG	20.5.90
--	Trooper	SLATER, CG	Unknown

Attested from
24.11.89 to 12.9.90

"B" TROOP

Officers

Captain FORBES, PW
Lieutenant SHEPSTONE, SWB
Lieutenant SLADE, CWP
Sub-Lieutenant MUNDELL, MHG
RSM BODLE, W

NCOs and Men

No	Rank	Name	Date Attested
1	TSM	LYONS-MONTGOMERY, FW	24.11.89
3	Sergeant	BRAY, R	10.12.89
4	Sergeant	FITZGERALD, EW	10.12.89
5	O/Room Sergeant	MORKEL, RA	18.12.89
6	Sergeant	VICKERS, JD	18.12.89

7	Sergeant	ADCOCK, RW	18.12.89
34	QMSergeant	HILLIER, JH	24.11.89
116	Sergeant	WILLIAMS, HG	4.1.90
20	Corporal	DAVIS, W	2.11.89
23	Corporal	DU PREEZ, DP	1.11.89
30	Corporal	GREEN, A	10.11.89
42	Corporal	KEANE, RNC	2.12.89
54	Corporal	MILLS, WT	10.12.89
68	Corporal	SWARTON, C	2.11.89
77	Corporal	VOIGHT, FJ	18.12.89
526	Corporal	BELL, B	14.5.90
2	Lance Corporal	SMITH, RAL	2.12.89
13	Lance Corporal	BOTTOMLEY, DP	10.12.89
63	Lance Corporal	SCOTT, JF	2.12.89
101	Lance Corporal	MORKEL, CF	3.1.90
41	Farrier	KAY, R	24.11.89
8	Trooper	ABBOTT, JJ	2.12.89
9	Trooper	ADAMS, T	2.12.89
10	Trooper	ARNOLD, HA	10.12.89
11	Trooper	BARTLETT, S	2.12.89
12	Trooper	BLYTH, WJ	24.11.89
15	Trooper	BURSTALL, JF	10.12.89
17	Trooper	CLARKE, WH	10.12.89
18	Trooper	COX, F	18.12.89
19	Trooper	DAVIS, H	10.12.89
21	Trooper	DONOHOE, A	24.11.89
22	Trooper	DOUGLASS, H	2.12.89
24	Trooper	ELSE, W	2.12.89
25	Trooper	ENRIGHT, GD	24.11.89
26	Trooper	FERMANER, GW	2.12.89
27	Trooper	FIELDS, RJ	10.12.89
28	Trooper	FISHER, D	24.11.89
29	Trooper	FLANAGAN, J	24.11.89
31	Trooper	HARDING, R	10.11.89
33	Trooper	HELLETT, H	2.1.89
36	Trooper	HOLMES, CB	24.11.89
37	Trooper	JACKSON, HJ	2.12.89
39	Trooper	JESSOP, E	24.11.89
40	Trooper	KANNEMEYER, F	2.12.89
43	Trooper	KENNEDY, J	24.11.89
44	Trooper	KERR, MJ	12.12.89
45	Trooper	KNEISER, H	24.11.89
46	Trooper	KNOX, P	24.11.89
49	Trooper	LE CORDEUR, M	18.12.89
50	Trooper	MANTHEY, J	10.12.89

51	Trooper	MARTELL, H	2.12.89
52	Trooper	MORGAN, W	10.12.89
53	Trooper	MITCHELL, JB	24.11.89
57	Trooper	PAYNE, FDA	22.11.89
58	Trooper	PROCTOR, R	24.11.89
59	Trooper	PURDON, FA	10.12.89
60	Trooper	RATHFELDER, F	2.12.89
61	Trooper	ROWLAND, AC	10.12.89
62	Trooper	SANDERSON, RH	10.12.89
64	Trooper	SCOTT, HNP	2.12.89
65	Trooper	SIMPSON, WB	2.12.89
67	Trooper	STEDLAR, C	2.11.89
59	Trooper	TREVOR, R	10.11.89
70	Trooper	TREVOR, J	24.11.89
71	Trooper	TURNER, DM	2.12.89
72	Trooper	THACKERAY, E	10.12.89
74	Trooper	VEALE, AJM	2.12.89
76	Trooper	VICARY, J	2.12.89
78	Trooper	WARNER, J	18.12.89
79	Trooper	WEBBER, BJ	10.12.89
80	Trooper	WILLIAMS, W	24.11.89
81	Trooper	WILLIAMS, H	10.12.89
82	Trooper	WHITE, FJ	24.11.89
83	Trooper	BURNS, J	18.12.89
97	Trooper	WIGNALL, TJ	18.12.89
104	Trooper	CULVERHOUSE, J	26.12.89
108	Trooper	SINCLAIR, AL	26.12.89
150	Trooper	FRASER, J	27.1.90
151	Trooper	PURSER, EA	27.1.90
215	Trooper	SISSING, CA	17.2.90
226	Trooper	SYMONS, FH	17.2.90
232	Trooper	STEWART, J	17.2.90
235	Trooper	PALMER, JA	20.2.90
259	Trooper	SHARPE, CE	20.2.90
274	Trooper	SAVILLE, H	21.2.90
296	Trooper	SAVAGE, W	22.2.90
461	Trooper	REID, J	10.4.90
469	Trooper	RICHARDS, H	31.3.90
474	Trooper	ST LEGER, K	31.3.90
483	Trooper	CAMPBELL, PW	1.4.90
484	Trooper	CHRISTISSON, TJ	1.4.90
485	Trooper	CORYNDON, RT	1.4.90
486	Trooper	CORNWALL, WL	1.4.90
487	Trooper	DURELL, A	1.4.90
488	Trooper	ELLIOTT, AWA	1.4.90

489	Trooper	EHLERT, F	1.4.90
490	Trooper	FEATHERSTONEHAUGH, HW	1.4.90
491	Trooper	GRIMMER, J	1.4.90
492	Trooper	MACROBERT, JM	1.4.90
493	Trooper	NESBITT, HW	1.4.90
494	Trooper	O'MEARA, BEA	1.4.90
495	Trooper	STEIR, WK	1.4.90
496	Trooper	SEWARD, GE	1.4.90
507	Trooper	REYNOLDS, WOH	30.4.90

**Attested from
24.11.89 to 12.9.90
"C" TROOP**

Officers

Captain KEITH FALCONER, C
Lieutenant BRACKENBURY, HV
Sub-Lieutenant CHAPLIN, E

NCOs and Men

No	Rank	Name	Date Attested
113	TSM	STEWART, JC	4.1.90
102	Sergeant	HOBSON, CR	3.1.90
129	Sergeant	NESBITT, RC	13.1.90
199	Sergeant	BOWLES, H	28.1.90
114	Lance Sergeant	QUORN, JC	4.1.90
88	Corporal	MARTIN, CB	18.12.89
94	Corporal	ROBERTSON, H	18.12.89
95	Corporal	TOURNAILLON, EH	18.12.89
96	Corporal	THOMPSON, JT	26.12.89
98	Corporal	MUIRHEAD, A	27.12.89
103	Corporal	ELIN, HD	26.12.89
120	Corporal	VAN DER BYL, CL	4.1.90
153	Corporal	EASTON, TJ	19.1.90
166	Corporal	ROBINSON, WH	19.1.90
32	Trooper	HEBERDEN, RC	18.11.89
38	Trooper	JENNINGS, MJ	24.11.89
73	Trooper	VAN DER BYL, GV	10.12.89
85	Trooper	HARRHY, EW	18.12.89
86	Trooper	HUGHES, JS	18.12.89
87	Trooper	JAMES, H	18.12.89
89	Trooper	MOFFAT, F	18.12.89
90	Trooper	MCGOWAN, JJ	18.12.89
99	Trooper	DAY, J	18.12.89

100	Trooper	ABERCROMBY, J	3.1.90
106	Trooper	MANNING, GA	26.12.89
107	Trooper	HANNAN, BJ	26.12.89
111	Trooper	BRABANT, JS	11.1.90
112	Trooper	SINGLETON, S	11.1.90
115	Trooper	SMYTHE, JE	4.1.90
119	Trooper	FIELDING, HC	4.1.90
121	Trooper	BIGG, JW	4.1.90
122	Trooper	RUSSELL, AC	4.1.90
124	Trooper	WESTPHAIL, J	4.1.90
127	Trooper	ROSS, A	4.1.90
130	Trooper	NESBITT, CS	13.1.90
132	Trooper	MCADAM, J	13.1.90
133	Trooper	TUCK, H ST J	13.1.90
135	Trooper	PRIESTLEY, F	13.1.90
136	Trooper	FICHARDT, EG	13.1.90
138	Trooper	BURTON, HH	13.1.90
139	Trooper	TORBET, F	13.1.90
140	Trooper	MCGILLVRAY, J	13.1.90
141	Trooper	FOWLES, C	13.1.90
143	Trooper	BENNETT, HJ	13.1.90
144	Trooper	NETTETON, GA	13.1.90
145	Trooper	HOBSON, C	13.1.90
152	Trooper	HALL, F	19.1.90
154	Trooper	HICKEY, FL	19.1.90
155	Trooper	HUDSON, HJ	19.1.90
156	Trooper	WISEMAN, RR	19.1.90
157	Trooper	CLARKE, D	19.1.90
159	Trooper	VENNELL, HR	19.1.90
161	Trooper	BLACK, A	19.1.90
162	Trooper	GLOVER, J	19.1.90
163	Trooper	DUNCAN, RW	19.1.90
168	Trooper	JESSIMAN, JJ	19.1.90
169	Trooper	MURPHY, GL	19.1.90
170	Trooper	TURNBULL, GF	19.1.90
171	Trooper	FEATHER	19.1.90
172	Trooper	THORNE, CJ	19.1.90
173	Trooper	CASPAR, GO	19.1.90
174	Trooper	TIQUIN, M	19.1.90
179	Trooper	GRIFFITHS, HG	28.1.90
200	Trooper	RODRIQUEZ, M	27.1.90
384	Trooper	LONG, E	27.2.90
416	Trooper	MCPARTLAND, J	24.2.90
422	Trooper	MOORE, J	24.2.90
432	Trooper	SPRING, HN	12.3.90

No	Rank	Name	Date
433	Trooper	ROSS, GP	14.3.90
434	Trooper	PATTERSON, R	14.3.90
435	Trooper	SINCLAIR, RD	14.3.90
436	Trooper	CLARKE, J	3.3.90
437	Trooper	MASON, WS	3.3.90
438	Trooper	NEWMAN, PJ	3.3.90
439	Trooper	ALLAN, JR	3.3.90
440	Trooper	GLASSEN, GH	3.3.90
441	Trooper	PLAYER, GJ	3.3.90
442	Trooper	WALSH, -	3.3.90
455	Trooper	DUNCAN, JL	19.3.90
467	Trooper	CONWAY, JMH	31.3.90
468	Trooper	ELLIOTT, HCD	31.3.90
472	Trooper	COLLINS, G	31.3.90
502	Trooper	RIELAND, CJ	4.5.90
503	Trooper	SCOTT	4.5.90
509	Trooper	ROBERTSON, AE	30.4.90
510	Trooper	HERBERT, E	30.4.90
511	Trooper	NEWTON, J	30.4.90
515	Trooper	COZENS, A	4.5.90
516	Trooper	LEWIS, J	4.5.90
517	Trooper	BARBER, AH	4.5.90

Attested from
24.11.89 to 12.9.90
"D" TROOP
Officers

Captain CHAMLEY-TURNER, E
Lieutenant CODRINGTON, RPJ
Lieutenant HICKS-BEACH, W
Lieutenant DUNCAN, RP

NCOs and Men

No	Rank	Name	Date Attested
314	TSM	CUNNINGHAM, WJ	13.2.90
190	Sergeant	VINCENT, W	28.1.90
237	Sergeant	COOPE, JCJ	7.2.90
335	Sergeant	WARREN, FJ	13.2.90
417	Sergeant	JUDGE, CE	24.2.90
191	Corporal	WITHERS, GB	28.1.90
315	Corporal	MUNDY, R	13.2.90
322	Corporal	HENRY, M	13.2.90
324	Corporal	HARPER, HA	13.2.90

331	Corporal	ROSS, WJ	13.2.90
463	Corporal	COOKE, EW	3.4.90
178	Lance Corporal	MADDEN, WJ	28.1.90
75	Trooper	VIZARD, GF	2.12.89
110	Trooper	ABRAMS, E	11.2.90
128	Trooper	WOLHUTER, GH	22.1.90
137	Trooper	HILLS, GH	13.1.90
148	Trooper	DURDEN, HV	24.1.90
177	Trooper	HILLS, GH	29.1.90
181	Trooper	DAWES, HV	28.1.90
182	Trooper	BRADBURN, C	28.1.90
183	Trooper	BUTT, C	28.1.90
184	Trooper	MCLUCKIE, C	28.1.90
185	Trooper	STRUTT, S	28.1.90
189	Trooper	RAYNER, H	28.1.90
192	Trooper	SMALLBERGER, C	28.1.90
193	Trooper	SMITHYMAN, TM	28.1.90
194	Trooper	GAIN, G	28.1.90
196	Trooper	GILL, TG	28.1.90
238	Trooper	HEINEMANN, JA	7.2.90
240	Trooper	WEALL, ME	7.2.90
241	Trooper	SNOWBALL, A	7.2.90
242	Trooper	ROWE, WJ	7.2.90
243	Trooper	HAYHILL, JA	7.2.90
244	Trooper	TIMEWELL, WA	7.2.90
245	Trooper	DUNN, W	7.2.90
246	Trooper	PARNELL, JC	7.2.90
247	Trooper	HUNTLEY, DH	7.2.90
248	Trooper	BARNES, TWF	7.2.90
249	Trooper	BARLOW, GF	7.2.90
250	Trooper	ALMOND, J	7.2.90
252	Trooper	WERRETT, JM	7.2.90
253	Trooper	INGRAM, WC	7.2.90
254	Trooper	POLNES, T	7.2.90
255	Trooper	FORRESTALL, P	7.2.90
256	Trooper	CHALMERS, J	7.2.90
276	Trooper	BROWN, HCW	21.2.90
316	Trooper	ABBOTT, WA	13.2.90
318	Trooper	ECKSTEIN, JW	13.2.90
319	Trooper	EBBAGE, WRL	13.2.90
320	Trooper	FREDMAN, W	13.2.90
321	Trooper	GATES, L	13.2.90
326	Trooper	LANDY, J	13.2.90
327	Trooper	MCLEOD, WJ	13.2.90
328	Trooper	MOLL, R	13.2.90

330	Trooper	ROACH, H	13.2.90
332	Trooper	STEWART, JT	13.2.90
333	Trooper	TAYLOR, JB	13.2.90
334	Trooper	VALLE, BW	13.2.90
336	Trooper	WILLIAMS, CW	13.2.90
415	Trooper	YOUNG, AL	24.2.90
418	Trooper	MURNEY, F	24.2.90
419	Trooper	ORPEN, AF	24.2.90
420	Trooper	SWEMMER, AL	24.2.90
421	Trooper	HEAD, E	24.2.90
423	Trooper	CLOWES, RCW	24.2.90
424	Trooper	GIBBON, GW	24.2.90
425	Trooper	HORWOOD, WR	24.2.90
426	Trooper	PEASE, DC	24.2.90
427	Trooper	LEES, JH	24.2.90
429	Trooper	WILLIAMS, J	24.2.90
431	Trooper	THOMAS, L	24.2.90
446	Trooper	DE VILLIERS, JJ	22.3.90
457	Trooper	HUGHES, A	2.4.90
458	Trooper	KEMP, S	10.4.90
459	Trooper	MCPHERSON, CG	10.4.90
460	Trooper	POWRIE, F	10.4.90
465	Trooper	SELBY, PH	3.4.90
466	Trooper	TAYLOR, FT	3.4.90
471	Trooper	TAYLOR, WM	31.3.90
475	Trooper	HUTCHINSON, F	31.3.90
477	Trooper	BROWN, W	31.3.90
478	Trooper	WHITTLE, CW	31.3.90
482	Trooper	DYER, HL	24.4.90
513	Trooper	GOTHE, N	4.5.90
518	Trooper	WHEATLEY, EM	4.5.90
519	Trooper	SAMPSON, J	4.5.90
520	Trooper	GRANT, RWE	4.5.90
521	Trooper	BEHN, O	3.5.90
587	Trooper	SEALE, E	9.9.90

**Attested from
24.11.89 to 12.9.90
"E" TROOP**

Officers

Captain LEONARD, AG
Lieutenant BRUCE, FW
Sub-Lieutenant GREY, AE

NCOs and Men

No	Rank	Name	Date Attested
501	TSM	HOLE, W	3.5.90
84	Sergeant	GORDON, JH	18.12.89
360	Sergeant	KIRKMAN, G	27.2.90
395	Sergeant	DILLON, CWC	1.3.90
556	Sergeant	CHINERY, LA	20.3.90
91	Corporal	MCGUINESS, CA	18.12.89
176	Corporal	KONIG, FW	29.1.90
302	Corporal	PARKER, AR	22.2.90
307	Corporal	LYNCH, WP	22.2.90
308	Corporal	MORONEY, H	22.2.90
311	Corporal	MALHERBE, WS	22.2.90
325	Corporal	O'MAKER,	24.2.90
329	Corporal	MURPHY, JJ	13.2.90
337	Corporal	ROBINSON, JMH	22.2.90
339	Corporal	FARMERY, EA	24.2.90
342	Corporal	SCHULTZ, H	24.2.90
343	Corporal	LLOYD, WR	24.2.90
344	Corporal	LLOYD, EG	24.2.90
345	Corporal	NIXON, H	24.2.90
348	Corporal	KIELSTROM, AW	22.2.90
351	Corporal	MORLEY, W	24.2.90
352	Corporal	MCLAGHLAN, R	22.2.90
353	Corporal	DESMIDT, W	27.2.90
357	Corporal	STANZLASS, G	27.2.90
358	Corporal	DIVINE, CH	27.2.90
366	Corporal	SHORT, H	27.2.90
368	Corporal	MORIATY, A	27.2.90
371	Corporal	PROMINTZ, F	27.2.90
376	Corporal	SNYMAN, JJ	27.2.90
377	Corporal	RAUTENBACH, S	27.2.90
380	Corporal	ROSS, W	27.2.90
390	Corporal	STEWART, T	1.3.90
391	Corporal	FITZGERALD, F	1.3.90
399	Corporal	SEYMOUR, G	4.3.90
401	Corporal	O'SHAUGHNESSEY, J	24.3.90
402	Corporal	SULLIVAN, T	4.3.90
404	Corporal	ROWLEY, A	4.3.90
408	Corporal	BUTLER, H	4.3.90
410	Corporal	BALL, J	4.3.90
411	Corporal	MOORE, H	4.3.90
412	Corporal	JAMES, G	27.2.90

414	Corporal	SMEE, J	4.3.90
454	Corporal	FLETCHER, R	26.3.90
481	Corporal	MCADAM, JC	24.4.90
504	Corporal	NOLAN, C	6.6.90
508	Corporal	BLUNDELL, AS	30.4.90
522	Corporal	RINGLEY, WD	3.5.90
524	Corporal	KNIGHT, HT	3.5.90
175	Trooper	FITZJOHN, AE	29.1.90
188	Trooper	VAN WYK, NL	28.1.90
301	Trooper	YOUNG, EF	22.2.90
303	Trooper	WHITE, W	22.2.90
306	Trooper	BERTRAM, CF	22.2.90
310	Trooper	JENKINS, A	22.2.90
313	Trooper	BUTLER, CA	22.2.90
338	Trooper	FINUCANE, E	24.2.90
340	Trooper	WHITE, S	24.2.90
341	Trooper	THORSON, M	24.2.90
346	Trooper	CHAMBERLAIN, CD	24.2.90
350	Trooper	YOUNG, RA	22.2.90
354	Trooper	JOHNSON, WA	27.2.90
356	Trooper	FITZSIMMONS, J	27.2.90
361	Trooper	BREDENKAMP, H	27.2.90
363	Trooper	EGAN, A	27.2.90
369	Trooper	COOK, J	27.2.90
370	Trooper	ELSKE, C	27.2.90
372	Trooper	BRIDGER, DD	27.2.90
374	Trooper	WRIGHT, F	27.2.90
375	Trooper	BARBER, P	27.2.90
378	Trooper	BRIDGER, JD	27.2.90
381	Trooper	VAN HEERDEN, H	27.2.90
382	Trooper	HACKWELL, H	27.2.90
383	Trooper	HULBERT, JH	27.2.90
384	Trooper	LONG, E	27.2.90
385	Trooper	JAMES, H	27.2.90
386	Trooper	FITZSIMMONS	27.2.90
388	Trooper	HUDSON, D	1.3.90
389	Trooper	DILLON, DC	1.3.90
392	Trooper	WESTBROOK, TP	1.3.90
393	Trooper	WOLD, J	1.3.90
396	Trooper	BRANNAN, F	4.3.90
400	Trooper	BURKE, CF	4.3.90
403	Trooper	HARDY, T	4.3.90
405	Trooper	GOLDSBURG, JT	4.3.90
407	Trooper	COOKE, W	4.3.90
409	Trooper	WILSON, C	4.3.90

No	Rank	Name	Date
443	Trooper	BRYNE, J	4.3.90
444	Trooper	HUNTER, J	6.3.90
464	Trooper	HYLAND, JP	3.4.90
480	Trooper	HENDRICK, J	24.4.90
523	Trooper	WHITEHEAD, AR	3.5.90
525	Trooper	THOMAS, WH	3.5.90
529	Trooper	WHITEHEAD, CL	14.5.90
531	Trooper	ATKINSON, WG	20.5.90
539	Trooper	CARDEW, CA	23.6.90

**Attested from
24.11.89 to 12.9.90**

LIST OF MEMBERS WHOSE TROOP IS NOT STATED

No	Rank	Name	Date Attested
14		BREMER, G	10.12.89
16		BUCHANAN, J	10.12.89
47		KRIGE, JD	4.12.89
55		MCROBERTS	24.11.89
66		SMITH, S	24.11.89
92		PINKERTON	18.12.89
93		RENNTER	18.12.89
105		MORRISON, J	26.12.89
109		LASS, A	13.1.90
117		COETZEE, P	4.1.90
118		MCCARTER, W	4.1.90
123		VENTER, H	4.1.90
125		WIENED, C	4.1.90
126		WENT, A	4.1.90
131		CONSTABLE, S	13.1.90
134		WHITE, C	13.1.90
142		KEENAN, C	13.1.90
146		DEWIT, JA	23.1.90
147		MCCARTHEY, G	23.1.90
149		PURCELL, W	24.1.90
158		MCKEON, E	19.1.90
160		EVERITE	19.1.90
164		HOLMER, S	19.1.90
165		GIBBS, HC	19.1.90
167		POWELL, E	19.1.90
183		BRETT, C	28.1.90
186		CROSSAN, T	28.1.90
187		TYSEN, CAFD	28.1.90
195		BERG, G	28.1.90

197	KEBL	28.1.90
198	POWER, JW	1.2.90
208	MCGRATH, J	15.2.90
217	BRAND, J	17.2.90
219	THOMPSON, J	17.2.90
221	CRADOCK, H	21.2.90
	FANGRENOL	17.2.90
224	LOGAN, J	17.2.90
228	THOMPSON, W	17.2.90
230	JOHNSON, S	17.2.90
231	SEYMOUR, T	17.2.90
239	PRINCEPS, EC	7.2.90
251	STEWART, JF	7.2.90
260	PHILLIPS, JH	20.2.90
264	PETERSON, H	20.2.90
282	MCGEE, J	21.2.90
283	CASEY, B	21.2.90
285	ANDREAN, A	21.2.90
293	GIBSON, A	21.2.90
304	MCKNIGHT	22.2.90
305	KENNEDY, J	22.2.90
309	JONES	22.2.90
312	JAMES	22.2.90
317	COULON, J	13.2.90
323	HILLBERG, F	13.2.90
347	HANSEN, C	13.2.90
349	WILLIAMS, H	22.2.90
355	LOTTERY	27.2.90
359	MACK	27.2.90
364	EVANS	27.2.90
365	CROSS	27.2.90
367	JOHNSON, WA	27.2.90
387	ANDERSON, J	1.3.90
394	TIMMINS	1.3.90
397	REARDON, M	4.3.90
398	MILLS	4.3.90
406	GRANT, C	4.3.90
413	RAY	1.3.90
430	DOBSON	24.2.90
455	DUNCAN	19.3.90
462	WALKER	6.4.90
479	SMITH	31.3.90
527	SMITH	14.5.90
532	FINDLAY	15.5.90
533	BOYDO, J	20.5.90

534	BURCHNALL, S	20.5.90
535	DAVENPORT, P	20.5.90
536	RICKETTS, A	20.5.90
537	ARMSTRONG, WL	1.7.90
538	WARRINGTON, FC	2.7.90
540	MORIER	23.6.90
541	KING, AW	22.7.90
542	MOODY, WJ	21.5.90
543	CARDEW	13.7.90
543	GIELGUD	6.7.90
545	CARTE	6.7.90
546	HOUSTON	22.6.90
547	WEBSTER	22.6.90
548	OBORN	1.7.90
549	MANSFIELD	17.6.90
550	AMERY	7.6.90
551	WHITE, J	17.6.90
552	RAWSTONE	17.6.90
553	GRACEY	12.8.90
554	RANDALL	12.8.90
555	TUPPER	14.8.90
556	GUERNEY	8.7.90
557	LUYARD, MA	15.7.90
558	REID, R	15.7.90
559	BRUCE, OR	15.7.90
560	DAVIS, WG	15.7.90
562	REID	9.9.90
563	ALLMAN	9.9.90
564	ARNOLD	9.9.90
565	BATES	9.9.90
566	BASSINGTHWAITE	9.9.90
567	BOARDMAN	9.9.90
568	BROWN	9.9.90
569	CHIVES	9.9.90
570	COLLIER	9.9.90
571	CLARKE	9.9.90
572	DREW, A	9.9.90
573	DU PLOY	9.9.90
574	EHLERT	9.9.90
575	ELIOT	9.9.90
576	FELTHAM	9.9.90
577	FITZMAURICE	9.9.90
578	FLECK	9.9.90
579	FORBES	9.9.90
580	GUNTHED	9.9.90

581	HOWEL	9.9.90
582	INGLESBY	9.9.90
583	MCMASTER	9.9.90
584	MIDDLEMASS	9.9.90
585	MILLER	9.9.90
586	ORTON	9.9.90
588	STEELE	9.9.90
589	SHAW	9.9.90
590	SNOW	9.9.90
591	SUTHERLAND	9.9.90
592	WEBB	9.9.90
593	WRIGHT	9.9.90
594	WOOD	9.9.90
595	WARRINGHAM	11.9.90
596	HOPPER	12.9.90
597	BARNARD, MW	12.9.90
598	GORDON	12.9.90
599	PITMAN	10.9.90
601	NORTON	12.9.90
606	HODGSON	11.9.90

www.ingramcontent.com/pod-product-compliance
Lightning Source LLC
Chambersburg PA
CBHW071202160426
43196CB00011B/2171